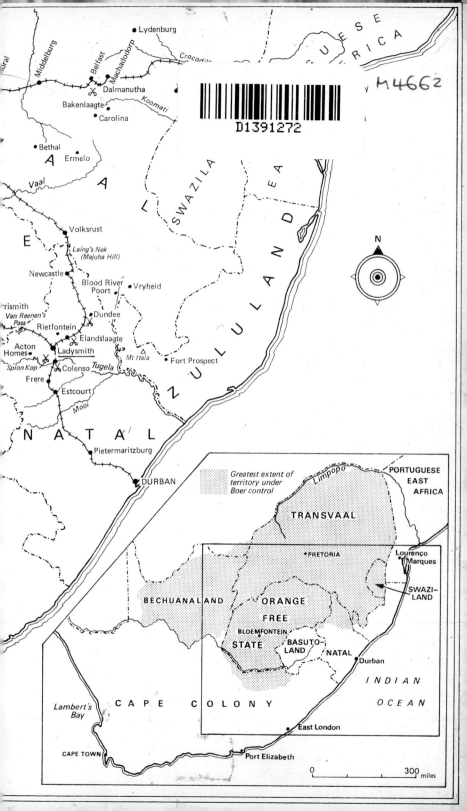

Lydenburg

Middelburg Belfast
Machadodorp
Dalmanutha

Bakenlaagte
Carolina

Koomati

Crocodile

M4662

D1391272

Bethal Ermelo

A

Vaal

A

E

Volksrust

Laing's Nek
(Majuba Hill)

Newcastle Blood River
Poort Vryheid

rismith
Van Reenen's
Pass Rietfontein Dundee

Acton Elandslaagte
Homes Ladysmith
Spion Kop Mt Itala Fort Prospect
Frere Colenso Tugela

Estcourt

Mooi

N A T A L

Pietermaritzburg

DURBAN

S W A Z I L A N D

Z U L U L A N D

E A

N

*Greatest extent of
territory under
Boer control*

Limpopo

PORTUGUESE
EAST
AFRICA

TRANSVAAL

•PRETORIA

Lourenço
Marques

BECHUANALAND

ORANGE

FREE

SWAZI-
LAND

BLOEMFONTEIN

STATE BASUTO-
LAND NATAL

Durban

I N D I A N

O C E A N

Lambert's
Bay

C A P E C O L O N Y

East London

CAPE TOWN Port Elizabeth

0 300 miles

THE BOER WAR

CONCISE CAMPAIGNS

General Editor: R. L. V. ffrench Blake

2

THE BOER WAR

EVERSLEY BELFIELD

LEO COOPER · LONDON

First published in Great Britain 1975 by
LEO COOPER LTD.
196 Shaftesbury Avenue, London WC2H 8JL

Copyright © 1975 by Eversley Belfield

ISBN 0 85052 192 0

Printed in Great Britain by
Ebenezer Baylis & Son Limited
The Trinity Press, Worcester, and London

CONTENTS

ILLUSTRATIONS

The author and publishers would like to thank the following for permission to reproduce illustrations in this book: Peter de Lotz, Nos. 4, 5, 6, 8, 10 and 11; The National Army Museum, Nos. 1, 2, 12, 15, 19 and 24.

MAPS

PREFACE

The Boer War possessed almost every ingredient necessary to establish it as a popular and romantic campaign. It can be regarded as an epic in which a Goliath, in the form of the British Empire at the peak of its strength, fought a tiny David-like figure, in the form of the two Boer Republics. Soon after this war began, the nineteenth century gave way to the twentieth and a year later, Queen Victoria died; the Boer War thus seemed designed to mark the end of an epoch.

In the Boer War, the conventional nineteenth-century conflict gives place, albeit uncertainly, to a guerrilla war, so foreshadowing a future pattern of combat. For perhaps the last time in the history of warfare, the man with his horse reigned supreme as the fighting unit, but it was also a war in which a machine, the railway engine, played an almost equally important role for the British. Militarily the Boer War was one of tremendous contrasts, opening with the three highly publicized sieges of Ladysmith, Kimberley and Mafeking, but soon developing, with the relief of Kimberley and the great de Wet hunts, into a campaign of endless mobility with soldiers marching hundreds and horsemen riding thousands of miles each year. However, at the same time, tens of thousands of others spent months cooped up in blockhouses. Although the set piece battles were few and relatively unimportant, they aroused international interest. Both sides can now be seen to have made the most incredible strategic blunders; the Boers, who after all lost the war, made the more serious ones at the outset, both by besieging the three towns and thereby tying up their troops unnecessarily, and also by not marching to Durban late in October, 1899 before the British reinforcements had arrived in Natal. As Smuts and many of the younger men realized at the time, the rapid seizure of the few ports of South Africa would have placed the British in an almost hopeless position.

In retrospect, probably the worst British strategic error was to have considered that the Boers were defeated after the capture of Pretoria. On the credit side, the Peace of Vereeniging was conciliatory and the reconstruction programme enlightened, although this did not reconcile many of the Boers for whom this struggle had latterly become a civil war. The total battle casualties were almost unbelievably light, far fewer than is now regarded as an acceptable toll on the roads of the bigger industrialized states. Particularly amongst the Boer women and children, the losses from disease in the concentration camps were far higher, but it is often forgotten that these non-combatants went there voluntarily, and at the insistence of their menfolk.

The Boer War was rich in personalities and some like Kruger, Rhodes and Roberts had gained international reputations before the outbreak of the conflict. In the course of the war, many others were to achieve renown and to continue their careers in a variety of fields. Amongst the famous Boers were soldier-politicians, Botha, Hertzog, Smuts, de la Rey and de Wet. The list of British names is impressive: Kitchener, French, Haig, Allenby, Plumer, Gough, Byng, Ian Hamilton and Baden-Powell amongst the soldiers. Like Winston Churchill, the young Edgar Wallace made his name there as a journalist, whilst Milner's 'Kindergarten' brought out many very able young men such as Leo Amery and John Buchan. Except for Kipling's poems and perhaps Deneys Reitz's *Commando*, this campaign resulted in no very memorable works of literature, but although overshadowed by the First World War, there are a considerable number of very readable memoirs, including Fuller's *Last of the*

Gentlemen's Wars. To add spice to the mixture, the Boer War also produced in Buller and Warren, a pair of classic military buffoons.

I hope to have shown that however incompetent the British Army may have been at the beginning, it emerged as a very much more efficient organization at the end of the campaign and this improvement was in large measure due to Kitchener's efforts. Finally, I have tried to present as objective an approach as possible to a conflict that can still arouse surprisingly strong partisan emotions.

I would like to thank my wife for her encouragement and for having done the preliminary work in preparing the maps. Colonel Val ffrench Blake, Mrs Diana Belfield and Major-General Eugene Strickland read the manuscript and made helpful criticisms. I am grateful to Miss Judy Colling-wood who, at short notice, typed the manuscript so accurately. In conclusion, I owe a great debt to the library staffs at the War Office, the Royal Military Academy, Sandhurst, the Prince Consort Library, Aldershot and my own university, Southampton.

EVERSLEY BELFIELD

Winchester, March 1975

LEADING PERSONALITIES
IN THE BOER WAR

The Conservative Government retained power throughout the period, winning the 'Khaki Election' of October, 1900.

BRITAIN

Marquess of Salisbury	Prime Minister
Joseph Chamberlain	Colonial Secretary
Marquess of Landsdowne	Secretary for War until October, 1900
Hon. St John Broderick	Secretary for War after October, 1900
Field-Marshal Viscount Wolseley	Commander-in-Chief
Sir Arthur Milner (later Lord Milner)	High Commissioner for South Africa and Governor of Cape Colony until January, 1901, and then Governor of Transvaal and Orange River Colonies
Sir W. F. Hely-Hutchinson	Governor of Natal, from January, 1901, Governor of Cape Colony
W. P. Schreiner	Prime Minister of Cape Colony to June, 1900

Sir Gordon Sprigg	Prime Minister of Cape Colony
*Sir Redvers Buller, V.C.	Commander-in-Chief South Africa to 16 December, 1899
*Field-Marshal Lord Roberts, V.C.	Commander-in-Chief South Africa to 29 November, 1900
*General Lord Kitchener (previously Chief-of-Staff to Lord Roberts)	Commander-in-Chief South Africa
*General Sir Ian Hamilton	Chief-of-Staff to Lord Kitchener from October, 1901

TRANSVAAL

Paul Kruger	President from 1883 to September, 1900
Schalk Burger	Acting President from September, 1900
Piet Joubert	Commandant-General until March, 1900
Louis Botha	Commandant-General

ORANGE FREE STATE

M. T. Steyn	President
J. Prinsloo	Commandant-General until December, 1899
A. M. Ferreira	Commandant-General until March, 1900
Christiaan de Wet	Acted as Commandant-General for the rest of the war

* Short biographies of these personalities will be found on the following pages.

BRIEF BIOGRAPHIES OF SOME
OF THE PROMINENT MILITARY
FIGURES IN THE BOER WAR

ALLENBY, F-M 1st Viscount, of Megiddo (1861–1936).
Commissioned into 6th (Inniskilling) Dragoons. 1884–8
served in expeditions to Bechuanaland and Zululand. Fought
throughout the Boer War with consistent success, latterly as
a column commander, becoming a colonel. 1915 commanded
V Corps and later Third Army. 1917 sent to Egypt to command and led the British to victory over the Turks in
Palestine and Syria. 1919–25 appointed Special High
Commissioner in Egypt.

BADEN-POWELL, Lt-Gen 1st Baron (1857–1941). Commissioned into 13th Hussars. Early specialized in 'scouting
and reconnaissance'. 1888–90 in Zulu War, 1895–6 in
Second Ashanti Campaign (W. Africa), returned to S. Africa
1896–7 for special duties in Matabeleland (Rhodesia). 1899
sent to S. Africa to form two regiments to protect Bechuanaland and Matabeleland. Achieved great fame as defender of
Mafeking, but less success later as a column commander
pursuing Christiaan de Wet. 1900 Milner entrusted him with
raising and training S. African Constabulary, a para-military
force. 1910 retired to devote most of the rest of his life to the
Boy Scouts Movement started in 1908 as a result of his
periodical *Scouting for Boys*. 1937 awarded Carnegie Peace
Prize.

BIRDWOOD, F-M 1st Baron, of Anzac & Totnes (1865–1951). Commissioned into 12th Lancers, very soon transferring into XI Bengal Lancers for economic reasons and remaining in India continuously for fourteen years. Served throughout the Boer War, first in Natal and then on Kitchener's staff accompanying him to India where he stayed until 1914, when sent to Egypt to command newly formed Australian, New Zealand Army Corps (ANZAC). Commanded ANZAC in Dardanelles with distinction. 1916–17 commanded 1st ANZAC on Western Front and later the Australian Corps. 1918 took over Fifth Army from Gough. 1925–30 Commander-in-Chief, India. 1930–8 Master of Peterhouse College, Cambridge.

BULLER, Gen Sir Redvers (1839–1908). Commissioned into King's Royal Rifle Corps (60th). 1873–4 First Ashanti War. 1878–81 South Africa winning V.C. 1879 in Kaffir War and 1881 in first Boer War. 1882–4 Egypt and Sudan. 1890–7 Adjutant-General. 1897–9 Commander-in-Chief, Aldershot Command, where active service formations stationed. 1899 Commander-in-Chief S. Africa. 1899–1900 Commander Natal Army. 1901 returned with Roberts to Aldershot Command but soon removed from there and retired.

BYNG, F-M 1st Viscount, of Vimy (1862–1935). Commissioned into 10th Hussars. Served throughout the Boer War, first commanding S. African Light Horse and later proving successful column commander, becoming a Colonel. 1910–12 Commander-in-Chief Eastern Command. 1912–14 in Command Egypt. 1914 3rd Cavalry Division. 1915 Cavalry Corps. 1915 sent from Western Front to Dardanelles where he organized the withdrawal. 1916–17 Canadian Corps, 1917–19 Third Army. 1921–6 Governor General of Canada. 1928–31 Chief Commissioner Metropolitan Police.

COCHRANE, Lt-Gen 12th Earl of Dundonald (1852–1935). Commissioned into Life Guards. 1884–5 in expedition that failed to relieve Gordon in Khartoum. 1899 went privately with own horses and servant to S. Africa and persuaded Buller to let him serve in Natal where he led a cavalry brigade. 1900 returned to England, retired 1907.

FRENCH, F-M 1st Earl of Ypres (1852–1925). 1866–70 in the Royal Navy. 1874 commissioned into 19th Hussars, via Suffolk Artillery Militia. 1884–5 in expedition that failed to relieve Gordon in Khartoum. 1899 with White in Ladysmith commanding the cavalry and left on the last train with Haig, then in command round Colesberg. 1900 commanded the cavalry division with Roberts' army in the relief of Kimberley and the capture of Bloemfontein and Pretoria. 1901 sent to Cape Colony to try suppress Boer rebels there. 1912–14 Chief of Imperial General Staff. 1914–15 commanded British Expeditionary Force until he resigned. 1916–18 Commander-in-Chief, Home Forces. 1918–21 Lord-Lieutenant of Ireland.

GATACRE, Major-Gen Sir William (1843–1906). Commissioned into the Middlesex Regt. Spent much of his early career in India displaying great zeal and bravery. 1898 commanded a brigade in the relief of Khartoum. His obsession for physical fitness led him to be nicknamed 'General Backacher'. 1898 Commander-in-Chief Eastern District. 1899–1900 commanded 3rd Division in Boer War losing battle of Stormberg and later dismissed by Roberts for incompetence; returned to be Commander-in-Chief Eastern District. Retired 1904 and died of fever while exploring Abyssinia.

GOUGH, Gen Sir Hubert (1870–1963). Commissioned into 16th Lancers. Served throughout the Boer War being severely wounded once and distinguishing himself as a dashing young lieutenant-colonel. 1915 divisional commander. 1916 1st Corps. 1916–18 V Army. 1919 Chief of Allied Mission to the Baltic.

HAIG, F-M 1st Earl, of Bemersyde (1861–1928). 1880–3 at Brasenose College, Oxford. Gained a pass degree but did not bother to receive it. Commissioned into 7th Hussars and soon singled out as exceptionally able. 1898 Omdurman. 1899–1900 Chief-of-Staff to French. 1900–02 column commander against the rebels in Cape Colony. Major-General at 43. 1906–07 helped Haldane in reorganization of the Army. 1909–11 Chief-of-Staff to C-in-C India. 1914 I Corps. 1915 First Army. 1915–19 Commander-in-Chief British forces on Western Front. 1919–21 Commander-in-Chief Home Forces. 1921 founded British Legion to assist ex-servicemen.

HAMILTON, Gen Sir Ian (1853–1947). Commissioned into Gordon Highlanders. 1881 badly wounded at Majuba Hill in First Boer War. 1882–90 ADC to Roberts. 1899–1900 in Ladysmith, then commanded a large column in Roberts' advance to Transvaal and then a division. 1900 returned to England as Roberts' Military Secretary. 1901 sent back to S. Africa to be Chief-of-Staff to Kitchener. One of the most highly considered soldiers in the Army. 1904–05 Chief of Military Mission to report on Japanese Army during Russo-Jap War. 1909–10 Adjutant-General. 1910–14 C-in-C Mediterranean Command in Malta. 1915 given command of disastrous Dardanelles landings and recalled, never to be re-employed.

KITCHENER, F-M 1st Earl, of Khartoum and Broome (1850–1916). Commissioned into Royal Engineers. 1878 surveyed Cyprus. 1885 with Wolseley in expedition that failed to relieve Gordon in Khartoum and stayed in Egypt and Sudan becoming commander of the Egyptian army. 1898 led expedition that gained victory over the Mahdi at Omdurman and retook Khartoum. 1899–1900 Chief-of-Staff to Roberts. 1900–02 C-in-C S. Africa. 1902–09 C-in-C India. 1911–14 British Agent and Consul General in Egypt and virtual ruler there. Probably the most prestigious British military personality since Wellington. 1914–16 Secretary of State for War. Drowned in HMS *Hampshire* when on a voyage to Russia.

LYTTELTON, Gen Sir Neville (1845–1931). Commissioned in Rifle Brigade. 1866 Canada to suppress Fernian rising. 1882 Egypt. 1898 Omdurman. 1899–1900 brigade commander Natal. 1900 divisional commander. 1900–01 in charge of forces for third de Wet hunt. 1902–04 C-in-C S. Africa. 1904–08 first Chief of Imperial General Staff. 1906–12 C-in-C Ireland. 1912–31 Governor of Royal Hospital, Chelsea.

METHUEN, 3rd Baron (1845–1932). Commissioned into Scots Fusilier Guards, later Scots Guards. 1873–4 First Ashanti Campaign. 1882 Egypt in battle of Tel-el-Kebir. 1884–5 Bechuanaland. 1899–1900 commanded 1st Division. Although very senior he served throughout the rest of the war largely devoting his efforts to trying to capture de le Rey in W. Transvaal. 1908–12 C-in-C S. Africa where he did much to improve relations with Boers. 1915–19 Governor of Malta.

PLUMER, F-M 1st Viscount, of Messines (1857–1932). Commissioned into York and Lancaster Regt. 1884 Egypt. 1893 sent to Natal and in 1896 to help quell the rising in Matabeleland (Rhodesia). 1899 raised the Rhodesian Horse. Served throughout the Boer War, proving one of the most successful column commanders, usually leading colonial troops; promoted brigadier. 1914 II Corps. 1915 Second Army. 1917 after Caporetto sent to Italy to command Allied forces there. 1918 recalled to France to lead Second Army during German Spring offensive. 1919–24 Governor of Malta. 1925–8 High Commissioner for Palestine and Trans-Jordan.

RAWLINSON, Gen 1st Baron, of Trent (1864–1925). Commissioned into King's Royal Rifle Corps later transferring to Coldstream Guards. ADC to Roberts in India. 1898 Omdurman. 1899 Ladysmith, then on Roberts' staff. 1901–02 successful column commander and promoted colonel. 1914 commanded IV Corps, originally helping withdrawal of Belgian Army. 1916–18 Fourth Army. 1919 in charge of Allied withdrawal from Archangel and Murmansk. 1920–25 C-in-C India.

ROBERTS, F-M 1st Earl (1832–1914). Commissioned into Bengal Artillery East India Company, 1858 won V.C. during Indian Mutiny. 1868 Abyssinian Campaign. 1878 First Afghan War. 1880 led the famous march from Kabul to relieve Kandahar in Afghanistan. 1885–93 C-in-C India. 1895 promoted Field-Marshal. 1895–9 C-in-C Ireland. December, 1899–1900 C-in-C S. Africa replacing Buller. January, 1901 returned to England for triumphant reception. 1901–04 C-in-C British Army until this post abolished and then Defence Council until 1905. Beloved by the soldiers more than almost any other commander in British history. Died when visiting Indian troops in France.

SMITH-DORRIEN, Gen Sir Horace (1858–1930). Commissioned into Sherwood Foresters. 1879 Zulu War. 1898 Omdurman. 1900 brigade commander under Roberts, later column commander until 1901. 1914–15 II Corps but dismissed by French and saw no further active service. 1918–23 Governor of Gibraltar.

GLOSSARY OF BOER WORDS

berg   a mountain

burg   a town, literally a borough

burgher   a male inhabitant of the Boer Republics possessing full political rights

bush   country covered in a varying degree with trees and undergrowth

donga   a cutting made on the surface of the ground by the action of water—sometimes filled with water, often dry

dorp   a village

drift   a ford

fontein   a spring, literally a fountain

inspan   to harness up

kop   a hill, literally head

kopje   a small hill

kraal   native village, or collection of huts, an enclosure for cattle

kranz, krantz or *krans*   cliff

laager   camp, bivouac

nek   a pass between two hills of any height

pan   a pond, full or empty; a saucer-like depression, usually dry in winter

poort   a gap, breaking a range of hills, literally gate

spruit   a watercourse, sometimes dry

veld   the country as opposed to the town; the open country

'Modern crusades have changed in name and object; they go to emancipate America with Lafayette, to liberate Greece with Fabvier; to defend the Boers with Villebois-Mareuil. Wherever a cry of distress rises, it is ever the same enthusiasm which carries them there, the same quest of a knightly ideal.'

> *From the introduction to the Diary of Colonel de Villebois-Mareuil, a retired Regular Officer adventurer and leader of the French Corps, killed at Tweefontein, 5 April, 1900.*

'Dear Teddy, I came over here meaning to join the Boers, who I was told were Republicans fighting Monarchists; but when I got here I found the Boers talked Dutch, while the Britishers talked English, so I joined the latter.'

> *From a letter written by an American, fresh from the Cuban War, to President Roosevelt, explaining his choice of sides.*

Beginning in 1899 and finishing in 1902, the Boer War linked two centuries, and this setting in time was remarkably symbolic. The earlier part of the campaign was largely fought according to the patterns of nineteenth-century military operations, whereas the latter and lengthier period of this war developed many modern characteristics, resembling the guerrilla conflicts that have become so prevalent in the twentieth century. Thus this war marked a watershed in the history of contemporary warfare. Nevertheless, the Boer War must be placed high in the long list of the world's unnecessary wars. Although deep-seated, the issues were relatively trivial and could and should have been settled without recourse to arms. This war was not concerned with the principle of white domination, but to decide which of the two groups, British or Boer, was to exercise mastery over South Africa. Paradoxically the Boer, having lost the war, soon gained the political ascendancy.

The Boer War still arouses emotional feelings. The importance of this relatively minor war cannot be explained by a superficial analysis of the casualties. The numbers killed in battle on both sides during the two and a half years of the campaign were less than 12,000, about 7,500 British and 4,000 Boers, but, when considering the importance of any war, statistics can prove a dangerous guide. This is especially true of the Boer War where the total casualties directly attributable to it were far higher, being about 44,000 of which 13,000 were British troops who died of disease, and 20,000 were Boer women and children who succumbed to disease in the concentration camps where they were interned. What for the British can be classified as a minor war was inevitably considered by the very small Boer nation to be a major event in their history. Yet for a variety of other reasons this remote and inconclusive war still retains a widespread hold on popular imagination and sentiment.

With both sides still feeling very conscious of being a minority in a newly conquered black world, the Boer War can almost be regarded as a civil war between two white races, and in some contemporary accounts British soldiers refer to their adversaries as Brother Boer. It has some parallels with the American Civil War, with few black people being directly involved. Like the Southerners, the Boers were fighting to preserve a way of life that they rightly felt was threatened by the influx of newer arrivals whose outlook and values were utterly different from theirs. In the later stages of the war, the British pursued a scorched earth policy like Sherman in Georgia. Unlike the American Civil War, however, neither side intended granting political concessions to the non-whites, but slavery had been abolished by the British in the Cape during the 1830s and the Boers had not introduced it into their new domains which they had settled by 1854. Another fundamental dissimilarity was that the Boers, unlike the Southerners, were pitted against a colonial power without whose support one of the adversaries, the local British, could never have considered taking up arms. The Boer leaders always hoped that the American Government would see mirrored in this struggle against the British Empire a sufficient resemblance to the American War of Independence to be moved to intervene on the Boer side. They also naïvely anticipated that other nations, especially the French and the Germans, would be aroused by their heroic contest to come to their assistance. They were to be bitterly disappointed by the lack of organized outside help for their cause and by the widespread support that Britain received from her colonies.

More paradoxically in the case of a long conflict that verged on being a civil war, the fighting was normally conducted in a civilized manner. In *The Last of the Gentlemen's Wars*, written thirty-five years after the Boer War, Major-General J. E. C. Fuller, the distinguished author and strategist, admitted that 'naturally there were black sheep on both sides' but stressed that 'by fighting in a sporting way we endowed the war with a chivalrous atmosphere'. On the Boer side, Deneys Reitz, in his book *Commando*, written immediately after the war, confirmed this opinion saying, 'Amid all the cruelty of the farm-burning, there was one redeeming feature in that the English soldiers, both officers and men, were unfailingly humane. This was so well known that there was never any hesitation in abandoning a wounded man . . . in the sure knowledge that he would be taken away and carefully nursed'. Fuller also emphasized that 'we never willingly waged war on women and children'.

A different picture was sometimes painted by contemporary civilian accounts written for home consumption. These highlighted the occasional atrocities. The large illustrated book *After Pretoria; the Guerrilla War* described an action in June, 1901. 'With their usual want of regard for their own womankind the enemy now proceeded to creep down on the British, using the wagons in which were their own wives and families as cover. No doubt they reckoned upon the well-known chivalry of the British for this was the regular practice of the Boers . . . It is needless to add that the Boers used not only expanding but also explosive bullets.' This work also gives the Boer version of this skirmish which was published in a German paper. This claimed that English soldiers had 'ordered the women and children to leave the wagons. Placing them in front of the soldiers, they shot between the women's arms upon the approaching Boers. Eight women and two children fell through the Boers' fire. When the Boers saw this they stopped firing. Yelling like wild beasts, they broke through the soldiers' lines beating to death the Tommies like mad dogs.' It was certainly true that, on this occasion, the Boers shot their prisoners.

CHAPTER ONE

The Country and its People

'There is no greater mistake possible than to think that any of us really understand the Boer.'

Sir Percy Fitzpatrick, December, 1899.

'The most priceless thing in the world was the life of the white man.'

General de la Rey.

The war was fought in parts of Cape Colony and Natal, both British colonies, and in the two independent Boer Republics, Orange Free State and Transvaal, then called the South African Republic. This region of 475,000 square miles consists of three distinct parts, a fairly narrow coastal strip, a high escarpment on the eastern side where the Drakensberg Mountains rise in places to over 10,000 feet and finally, a huge upland plateau covering most of Orange Free State and Transvaal known as the High Veld, about 4,500 feet above sea level. Although there are several large rivers, with many tributaries, none of them are navigable and all are liable to sudden flooding, which hampered operations and made the few bridges of great military value. Hardly any metalled roads existed and thus the railway system, at first almost everywhere single-tracked, greatly influenced the course of the war. The five main lines were the Western Railway from Cape Town to Rhodesia which runs alongside the Orange Free State and Transvaal borders for about 600 of its 1,350 miles. The Central Railway covers 750 miles from Port Elizabeth to Pretoria, via Bloemfontein and Johannesburg, and is connected to the Western Railway at De Aar. A third line comes from East London, via Stormberg, to join the Central Railway at Springfontein. Fourthly, passing through Colenso and Ladysmith, the Natal Railway joins Durban to Johannesburg, a distance of nearly 500 miles. Finally the Delagoa Bay line runs due west for 475 miles from Lourenço Marques, on the coast of Portuguese East Africa, to Pretoria; this was Transvaal's life-line since it nowhere passed through British territory.

The climate is fairly extreme. From October to March the daytime temperatures become very hot and, in the pure clear air, distances are most deceptive, visibility being far greater than in Europe. The nights are usually cold. Even in the summer thunderstorms are not infrequent, while the winters are wet and cold, soon turning the dirt roads into seas of mud and restricting movement. In the summer the veld could be used freely by military convoys which kicked up clouds of dust making unobserved movement impossible. Many small rocky hills, called kopjes, rise several hundred feet above the flat bushy ground providing excellent observation and strong points.

The economy of South Africa was then a predominantly rural one and thus the British had to import most of their military requirements; although tens of thousands of horses were bought locally, over 352,000 more horses and 104,000 mules had to be shipped to the war. Almost all the oxen were obtained in South Africa. With over 1,000 transport vessels employed at one time or another, Britain's naval supremacy enabled her to send supplies without fear of hindrance by outside powers.

The population of South Africa was then just over 5 million and was divided into four racial elements. In Natal lived about 100,000 Indians who were brought in after 1860, for the most part for agricultural work which the natives refused to do. Mainly in Cape Colony dwelt 300,000 coloureds, people of mixed blood. The biggest racial group were the African tribes known as Kaffirs, totalling about 3½ millions. The non-whites were not employed as soldiers, but both sides used them extensively as drivers, servants, messengers and guides; over 10,000 served with the Boers, and many more with the British who eventually armed some Scouts for their self-protection. Finally, the white population numbered about 1,100,000 and was divided into two almost equal groups. The slightly smaller section was composed of the predominantly British-speaking people who lived principally in the towns, of which Johannesburg was the largest. The Boers were mainly of Dutch or French Huguenot stock and, unlike the more recently arrived British settlers, had mostly ceased to have close ties with their European ancestors. Most of them hated town life, preferring to live a patriarchal existence with their large families on isolated farms, many of over 2,000 acres. The Boers then embodied in their make-up an unusually strong mixture of the far-sighted and the narrow-minded, the brave and the cowardly. Steeped in the Old Testament, their uncompromising spirit of racialism resembled that of the Jews.

Sir Percy Fitzpatrick had been born in Cape Colony and became a leading figure in Johannesburg business circles. He probably came as close as any outsider could to comprehending the Boer mentality. He wrote, 'The old-type Boer is by nature a sort of exclusive secret society. We cannot enter into his mind any more than we can into that of an Oriental or a native. There are times when they seem to go against every kind of reason or instinct or interest—as we understand things . . . The younger generation . . . are influenced by the things we understand—education, frank racialism of a simpler kind.' Small, young nations normally possess a highly developed and almost mystical sense of their own history. As de la Rey, the famous guerrilla leader explained, 'The Great Trek took our people inland and we occupied all this country which is now the Free State and Natal. We had to defend ourselves at every stage . . . the Boers would not sacrifice the life of a white man, not even for murder, cowardice or treachery . . . even those that were bad ones could still do something else; they could at least rear their families and increase our numbers.' This deep-rooted instinct influenced the Boers in the way they fought, nearly always preferring surrender to death. It also seems to have affected the British troops who often surrendered easily knowing that, as fellow white men, they would be well treated by their captors. In marked contrast, an utterly different attitude towards life existed among the African tribes, whom the British and Boers had been accustomed to fighting. The natives usually tortured anyone who fell into their hands and the Boers were equally ruthless, finding it hard to regard Kaffirs as human beings, in the white sense of the word, and they had little mercy on any black they captured helping the British.

CHAPTER TWO

The Causes of the War—
Mobilization

'I have but one great object in this world—that is to maintain the greatness of the British Empire . . . I firmly believe that in doing so I work in the cause of Christianity, of peace, of civilization, and the happiness of the human race generally.'

Lord Wolseley, Commander-in-Chief, British Army.

'You know how the Lord transplanted this people to this country and led it here amid miracles; so that we should have to say, "Lord, I no longer believe in Thee", if things came to such a pass with us that now, when thousands of enemies are assailing us, we voluntarily surrendered the land which He gave us.'

President Kruger of Transvaal.

Profound differences of opinion still exist about the rights and the wrongs of the events that led to the Boer War, but at the risk of over-simplification, three major causes will be briefly examined. The first cause lay in the Boers' belief in the righteousness of their case against the British, whom many regarded with a mixture of hatred and contempt. These explosive sentiments were fostered by the opinion of most Boers that they were engaged in an unfinished struggle against a greedy imperialistic power that had forced an innocent and God-fearing body of farmers first out of the Cape and then out of Natal. When, in 1854, the British had recognized both Orange Free State and Transvaal, this

5

danger appeared to have ended. But this proved an illusion because, in 1877, the Transvaal was peacefully annexed by the British at the request of the Boer settlers. Their country was bankrupt and the scattered white inhabitants were threatened with extinction by the risings of incensed native tribes who resented their lands being expropriated. Having successfully suppressed the native risings in the Zulu War of 1879, the British governed with little regard for the Boer traditions of democracy, and the Transvaalers rose up in 1880 to fight the First Boer War. After a series of skirmishes, a small, badly-led British force was defeated by Joubert at Majuba Hill on the Transvaal–Natal border in March, 1881. A legend was then created that under South African conditions the Boers could always beat the inefficient red-coated British soldiers. In 1881, under the Pretoria Convention, a peace very favourable to the Transvaal was granted by Gladstone's Liberal government. This was construed as proof of British readiness always to opt out of any expensive military operations there—a view that was reinforced by the London Convention of 1884, which the Transvaal claimed gave them complete independence from the British.

The second important factor arose out of the discovery of vast quantities of gold near Johannesburg during the late 1880s, which suddenly transformed the Transvaal from a very poor into a very rich country. The Boers did not mine the gold, but let the concessions to foreigners, known as Uitlanders. Mainly of British or colonial extraction, the Uitlanders were proud of their ancestry. Like all gold rushes, this one attracted many adventurers, rough, violent men who were supported by the diamond magnate, Cecil Rhodes, and others desirous of overthrowing the often corrupt administration of Pretoria. The Uitlanders considered that they were being discriminated against because they were denied any voting rights, and, despite paying nearly all the taxes, were also expected to defend the country against outside enemies, which could only mean the British. Organized by Rhodes, then Prime Minister of Cape Colony, the Jameson Raid of

1 and 2 Two senior British generals who fought throughout the campaign. (*Left*) Lt-General Lord Methuen who was de le Rey's adversary for most of the war; (*right*) Lt-General the Hon N. G. Lyttelton, later C-in-C South Africa and the first CIGS.

3 The eighteen Orange Free State Commandants with President Steyn (*centre, middle row*), Major Albrecht, the regular German artillery officer (*extreme left, middle row*) and the State Attorney Dickson (*extreme left, back row*). This picture was taken before the outbreak of the war.

4   A picquet of the 9th Lancers at Magersfontein; note the lances
which are most unsuitable weapons for fighting horsemen armed with
rifles.

December, 1895, aimed at persuading the Uitlanders to stage a coup to overthrow the Transvaal Government. The raid proved a fiasco. For all their boastings, the Uitlanders were ill-organized and not prepared to risk a rising, and the Boers easily captured Jameson and his 600 followers. The Jameson Raid marked a turning-point in South African history. The Boers believed that there had been collusion between Joseph Chamberlain and Rhodes, and the prospect of war between the two countries became increasingly probable. The failure of the raid made Transvaal more self-confident because it gained almost universal support and sympathy, particularly in the hitherto uncommitted Orange Free State, while the majority of Cape Boers, under the influence of a semi-secret society called the Afrikander Bond, displayed strong anti-British and pro-Transvaal sentiments. The famous telegram of support from the Kaiser was construed as a token of likely backing from the outside world. From 1896–9 the Transvaal openly re-armed, importing 80,000 modern rifles and 80 million rounds of ammunition, re-equipping their army with the most modern French and German guns and recruiting professional foreign officers for their artillery.

The third main cause for this war sprang from an intense personal antagonism which developed between President Kruger and Sir Alfred Milner. By 1899, Kruger, then aged 74, had been President and virtually undisputed ruler of Transvaal for 16 years; he controlled the administration largely through imported Dutch officials who negotiated lucrative, and often corrupt, concessions for the foreign firms exploiting the wealth of the country. In the Volksraad, or Parliament, Kruger abused his immense prestige, crushing and terrifying anyone who opposed him, including Joubert, de la Rey and, for a time, Louis Botha. When Britain granted independence to Transvaal in 1881 it was agreed that white residents should have equal voting rights, but then there had been very few non-Boer whites; by 1899, however, the Uitlanders outnumbered the burghers. Although conceding that these outsiders might have the vote, Kruger imposed so

2

many restrictions as to make the franchise almost impossible to obtain, nor would he countenance Uitlanders being elected to the Volksraad. Any British claim that white men with five to seven years' residence in Transvaal should automatically have the vote was classed by Kruger as interference in the internal affairs of a sovereign state and therefore unacceptable.

In 1897, Milner, aged 45, was appointed High Commissioner in South Africa and granted considerable powers by Joseph Chamberlain, the very influential Colonial Secretary. Where Kruger was narrow, bigoted and a passionate nationalist, Milner was highly educated and urbane but an intransigent imperialist. Where Kruger regarded the simple patriarchal Boer society as a God-given mode of life, Milner could envisage no more desirable existence for a people than to live under the protection of the British flag; he also considered Britain in duty bound to intervene where its citizens sought help when deprived of their just rights.

At first Milner genuinely hoped to persuade Kruger to give in and grant, with adequate safeguards, the vote to those Uitlanders who had lived in Transvaal for a reasonable period, but he soon became disillusioned with Kruger's tortuous methods of negotiating. On 31 May, 1899, the two men met at Bloemfontein where, under the Chairmanship of President Steyn, a final effort was made to reach a compromise on the Uitlander question. After five days of apparently fruitless negotiations, Milner broke off the conference and departed, just before receiving a telegram from Chamberlain urging patience. Some further proposals were bandied about during June, July and August, but all soon failed and the speeches by the leaders of both sides became more and more hostile. By September war seemed inevitable as each side persuaded itself that the other was about to attack. The vital question was who would be the first to strike.

From June to October, 1899, both sides prepared for war. The Boer Republics had less need to do this openly because, with an army that could be mobilized in a few days, they were on an almost permanent war footing. The organization of their forces was simplicity itself. In both the Transvaal and the Orange Free State every man between 16 and 60, with very few exceptions, was liable to unpaid military service, regarded by most as a voluntary rather than an imposed burden. The Boer citizen soldier was expected to report for duty with ten days' rations, a pony, a rifle and 30 rounds of ammunition; no uniforms existed, so he fought in his everyday clothes. In wartime, the major formation was the Commando which was based on the number of burghers in the electoral districts (22 in Transvaal and 18 in Orange Free State), they were sub-divided into wards, two for the smallest and five for the largest district. The size of the Commando varied from about 300 to 3,000 men. Even in the largest, like Pretoria, the military chief or Commandant was elected, which was symbolic of the democratic, pioneer spirit still prevailing. The most important officials were the Field Cornets; these local men were elected in each ward for three years and were supposed to keep a register of their burghers and see that their men were properly equipped. On mobilization, they were responsible for civil and military functions in the wards, such as the distribution of arms and ammunition (new Mausers were available for most burghers), and the requisitioning of necessary transport. To assist them, one or more Assistant Field Cornets were elected, each being responsible for 150–250 men. Below them were the corporals, also elected, who obtained all the necessary daily supplies for about 25 men. Having assembled and equipped all the men of their wards at the local towns, the Field Cornets then led them to the Commando rendezvous, the district capital from which the whole formation took its name.

The only two permanent contingents consisted of the Artillery and the Police. Including Reservists, the Artillery in Transvaal numbered about 800 and in Orange Free State 400 men. These gunners were well trained and commanded by competent foreign officers, and had about 100 guns, 75 being modern weapons of various calibres. The South African police, or ZARPs, and the much smaller Swaziland Police were para-military organizations trained and organized on army lines with their own officer corps, and amounted to about 1,500 men.

The *Official History* lists the grand total of Boers and their supporters under the following categories (Vol. I, p. 459):

Burghers of S.A.R. (South African Republic)	41,650
Burghers of O.F.S. ...　　...　　...　　...	27,609
Regular Forces, ZARP, Artillery ...　　...	2,686
Foreign Corps　　...　　...　　...　　...	2,120
Rebels, nearly all Cape Boers　　...　　...	13,300
	87,365

The Times History estimate was much lower, 60,000–65,000 (Vol. II, p. 88). Neither figure includes those under 16 and over 60, nor the women who occasionally took part in the fighting.

When the war began, some Boers responded unwillingly: Viljoen, Commandant of the lukewarm Johannesburg District, recalled that, 'Many malingerers suddenly discovered acute symptoms of heart disease and brought easily obtained doctor's certificates'. Those who refused to serve might be fined, but seldom were. Discipline was hard to enforce and hundreds of unenthusiastic men attached themselves to depôts and hospitals, or found non-combatant jobs. Leave was a perennial problem, burghers being entitled to it after three months' service, and many took it with or without permission, their reasons often being to supervise their farms or to rest and refit. Nevertheless, the two Boer Republics could be expected to put almost 50,000 mobile, resourceful soldiers into the field soon after the outbreak of any conflict. In addition, Milner reckoned that about half the 40,000 male Cape Boers would flock to the enemy at the first favourable opportunity, an opinion widely held in Transvaal, where 40,000 Martini-Henry rifles had been bought for them.

In June, 1899, the British forces were split between Natal and Cape Colony and amounted to under 10,000 men. A little later, ten fairly senior officers were sent out, including Colonels Baden-Powell and Plumer who both raised small white units in Rhodesia. On 8 September the Cabinet authorized the Regular troops in South Africa to be increased by 10,600, over half to come from India, partly because it was closer to Natal and partly because these units were at full strength. On 22 September it was finally decided to mobilize and send to South Africa, under Buller, an Army Corps of 47,000 men. But when war broke out, the British could only muster 27,000 troops, of whom 8,500 were local volunteers, such as the 1,000-strong Cape Mounted Police and the elite Uitlander Imperial Light Horse with 500 men. Until December therefore, when the Army Corps would be arriving, the Boers could be sure of outnumbering the British. Moreover, nearly all the Boers were mounted, whereas the British, though Regulars, were mainly infantrymen, and thus ill-trained for the type of warfare in which they were about to be engaged. Finally, the British suffered from the grave handicap of not knowing the country and having no accurate maps.

The decision in September to reinforce the garrisons in South Africa was interpreted by the Boers as conclusive evidence of Britain's intention to go to war. The two Republics already knew that preparations were being made to mobilize an Army Corps and may have been aware that contingency plans existed in the War Office to invade their territory. Undoubtedly, both Chamberlain and Milner were as keen on fighting as were most of the Boers. Contemporary evidence nevertheless does suggest that the decision in September to despatch troops was a purely defensive measure and designed to protect Natal and Cape Colony from invasion. The Army Corps could provide no short-term threat to the Boers because only on 22 September were preparations begun to activate it for overseas service by organizing its transport system and arranging for shipping. Not until 7 October were the Reservists who formed nearly half its manpower called out. The British actions must therefore be seen as a clumsy mixture of bluff and threat, not posing any real danger to the Republics before December at the earliest.

From 1899 Kruger increasingly left the direction of Transvaal policy to his 29-year-old State Attorney, J. C. Smuts. By September, this brilliant young Cambridge-trained lawyer was convinced that war with Britain was inevitable and was determined that the Boers should exploit their advantages from the outset. Smuts drew up a daring plan for the Boer forces to drive at once for the coast, aiming to seize Durban first and later Cape Town; having reached the coastal areas, Smuts argued that the British would not be able to land their troops at ports held by their adversaries. He stressed the need for speed whilst the Boers still had the numerical superiority, but Smuts' brilliantly conceived offensive made little appeal to the elderly men who led the Boer forces at the outbreak of war.

The Boer preparations surprised even some of the British who were on the spot. Captain O'Meara of the Royal Engineers, who had been mapping and surveying Cape Colony and Orange Free State since July, wrote that on 27 September, 'my astonishment on that evening was great, for I witnessed the arrival of the Winburg Commando. I had passed along 36 miles of road with everyone professing *peace*, yet the country had already commenced to collect its dogs of war . . . my desire to return at once and warn Kimberley's commander was intense; however, English people at Boshof assured me I would be shot if found travelling across country on a bicycle in the dark; so I deferred my departure till daybreak . . . Once I was astride my saddle I travelled 12 miles an hour, without once looking behind me!'

Smuts (like the British Government) had drafted an ultimatum which he intended should be rejected. Its most humiliating clauses were 'That the troops on the borders of the Republic shall be instantly withdrawn. That all reinforcements of troops which have arrived in South Africa since 1 July, 1899, shall be removed. That Her Majesty's troops which are now on the high seas shall not be landed in any part of South Africa.' Although prepared on 27 September, when the Transvaal Commandos had been mobilized, the delivery of this 48 hours' ultimatum was postponed until 9 October. This was mainly because Orange Free State forces were not ready, but also because of administrative difficulties encountered by Transvaal troops, such as shortages of wagons and lack of advanced ammunition depots. On 11 October the ultimatum expired and Britain was at war with two Republics. Early spring was chosen because the Boer horses and oxen could be sure of plentiful grazing as they advanced into Natal. For the British, the fortnight's delay over the ultimatum had been invaluable, giving them a chance to deploy the troops arriving in Natal and to make hasty preparations along their 1,000 miles of border with Transvaal and Orange Free State. 27,000 British Regulars and South African troops of British descent, together with 1,500 Rhodesians and a few hundred sailors, say 30,000 in all, now faced a Boer army whose size had been estimated at from 38,000 (*Times History*) to 48,000 (*British Official History*); undoubtedly the Boers outnumbered the British by about 10,000 men. This was to be Britain's first war against a white race since the Crimean War of 1853–6. Without any allies to be considered, the nation was bursting with enthusiasm and self-confidence, many people thinking that it would be ended by Christmas; the song 'Goodbye Dolly Gray' echoed popular feeling.

CHAPTER THREE

The Battles before Lady-smith and the Sieges

'There was not a man who did not believe that we were heading straight for the coast and it was well that the future was hidden from us and that we did not know that our strength and enthusiasm would be frittered away in a "meaningless siege".'

Deneys Reitz, Commando.

'The war will be over in a fortnight. We shall take Kimberley and Mafeking and give the English such a beating in Natal that they will sue for peace.'

Chief Justice Gregowski of Transvaal.

The major Boer offensive was directed against Natal, their nearest outlet to the sea, where a deep salient climbs up through the Drakensberg Mountains to penetrate almost to the veld of Transvaal and Orange Free State. On 12 October 14,000 Transvaalers began to move south down the road and railway that cuts through Laing's Nek, their first main objective being the rail junction of Ladysmith about 110 miles distant. Assembling to converge on Ladysmith from the west through Van Reenen's Pass were at least 6,000 Free Staters under Chief Commandant Marthinus Prinsloo, but they did not move until 18 October.

The Transvaalers were led by the cautious 65-year-old Commander General Joubert ('Slim-Piet'), who had always opposed the war; he was accompanied by his wife who

wielded considerable influence over him. The long colum.....
soon passed Majuba Hill where, 18 years earlier, Joubert
had defeated the British in the First Boer War. No opposition
was met during the leisurely 30 miles march to Newcastle,
occupied on 15 October, nor were there any demolitions,
the rail tunnel at Laing's Nek and the bridges over the rivers
being all left intact by the British.

On 7 October Lt-General Sir George White, V.C., a 64-
year-old veteran of the Mutiny and many other campaigns in
India, arrived in Natal. Given no instructions, and with some
of his formations still *en route* from India, White was
immediately confronted with an extremely complex and
unstable situation demanding rapid and irrevocable decisions.
White was faced with three choices. First he could withdraw
all his troops south of the Tugela River to repulse any Boer
thrust towards Pietermaritzburg and Durban. Milner and the
Governor of Natal strongly opposed such an abandonment of
territory, fearing its adverse effect on the morale of the pro-
British and its encouragement for the Cape Boers. Nevertheless this plan was advocated for military reasons by Colonel
Rawlinson, one of White's principal staff officers. Secondly,
White could try to hold the Boers as far from the frontier as
possible and hope to inflict a major defeat on them as soon as
possible; this proposal was passionately supported by his
predecessor, Major-General Sir Penn Symons, who had
already taken 4,000 troops to Dundee about 20 miles south of
Newcastle. Lastly, he could concentrate his troops in Ladysmith, a town unsuited to withstand a siege, but where 60
days' supply of stores had been accumulated. After considerable hesitation, he was jockeyed into this last and very
controversial choice, but before this siege started, three minor
engagements and one battle were fought.

The first engagement of the war was fought at Talana
Hill, just outside Dundee which was well stocked with
provisions. Symons had eventually persuaded White, already
at Ladysmith with 8,000 troops, to allow him to make a stand
there, although it meant splitting the British forces. Dundee

was an almost impossible place to protect, being surrounded by hills; a French officer described it as like being inside a chamber pot. However, Symons was confident that his Brigade, composed mostly of Regulars, could defeat several times their number of Boers, should they dare to attack him, which he doubted. Early on 20 October Dundee camp was shelled by Boers, under Lukas Meyer, 3,500 of whom had occupied the nearby Talana Hill during the night. Symons' forces responded quickly, but their counter-attack up the hill faltered and the General spurred his men on with that reckless courage so often displayed by officers, 11 out of the 51 killed at Talana being officers. Although mortally wounded, Symons' action had the desired effect and the infantry rushed up the hill in a frontal attack to capture it. General Yule now took over command. The artillery, which had previously been most effective, shelled the infantry when they reached the crest and temporarily drove them off it. In the early

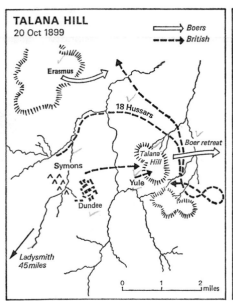

afternoon a truce was arranged; most of Meyer's men having escaped, the British soldiers returned to Dundee.

The battle was not quite finished. Symons had previously ordered Colonel Moller, with most of the 18th Hussars, to harass the retreat of the Boers. The cavalry moved round and were well placed to do this, but Moller awaited precise orders that never came and missed an excellent opportunity to disperse the Boer ponies and their guards when their riders were engaged in the battle. Finding himself about to be engulfed by the retreating Boers, Moller tried to extricate the rest of his force by going north, but was soon lost. He ran into some of General Erasmus' men, 2,000 of whom had spent the day quietly on a hill about four miles away from the battle and, after a brief resistance, Moller surrendered. British losses totalled 500, including 215 Hussars, while the Boers had about 150 casualties. Talana was an inconclusive victory against very mediocre Boer opposition.

News of Talana emboldened White to strike at an isolated Boer force under a subordinate of Joubert's, General Kock. He was told to take and hold a pass west of Dundee, but some of his German Corps advanced a further 20 miles and, on the evening of 19 October, captured a supply train at Elandslaagte Station, 10 miles north-east of Ladysmith. By 20 October this cosmopolitan contingent of some 800 men, including 140 Germans (mainly Uitlanders supporting the Republics' cause) and 70 Hollanders (Dutchmen working on contract for the Transvaal government) were astride the British lines of communication to Dundee.

On 21 October General French, the newly arrived cavalry commander, moving by road and rail, surprised Kock's men and recaptured the Station. But with 750 men he could not retain it for long, especially as Kock had two guns which were very well served throughout the battle. French asked White for reinforcements and these were rapidly despatched under the dashing Colonel Ian Hamilton, personally chosen by White on whose staff he was serving. Believing that the British had departed, the Boers relaxed.

When French, now reinforced, returned, they were surprised, but quickly recovered and, after some skirmishing, ensconced themselves along a low horseshoe-shaped ridge straddling the railway. This isolated force was now confronted with 1,300 cavalry, 550 gunners with 18 pieces of artillery and about 1,600 infantry. Before the attack, Hamilton made an inspiring speech and his soldiers cheered him, shouting 'We'll do it, sir. We'll do it'. The plan was for a frontal attack with artillery support, against the hills west of the Station where Kock had now concentrated his force. Supported by most of the cavalry, a larger force was to take the Boers from the flank; the rest of the cavalry was to be held back and only be unleashed when the Boers began to retreat.

Aided by a darkened sky and by their newly introduced khaki uniforms, those making the frontal attack were well concealed when they halted to await the flank attack. This met with severe opposition, but the heavy thunderstorm that broke enabled the troops to gain the edge of the plateau. As the sky cleared, the Boers resolutely defended the rest of the hilltop and the attack faltered. Appreciating the critical situation, Hamilton dashed across to rally the troops and, ordering the bugle sound, led the ensuing bayonet charge. Heavily outnumbered, most of the Boers fled and, when it was almost dark, a white flag appeared. Hamilton ordered the 'ceasefire' to be sounded but, either ignoring it or not realizing that the fighting had been ended, some 50 Boers launched into a desperate counter-attack which so disconcerted the British that it looked as if the infantry would be driven off the hill in confusion. But with effective artillery fire once more given, Hamilton again rallied his men, while French personally ran forward to stem the flight of any waverers, and the Boers were overwhelmed.

Some of the British cavalry, who were concealed behind the Boer positions, charged these disorganized troops, using lances and swords to great effect. The Boers complained that the cavalrymen did not always heed their offers of surrender, but it is impossible to stop such charges to take individual prisoners. The Boers henceforward hated the British cavalry. With 67 dead, 108 wounded and 188 prisoners the Boers lost more heavily at Elandslaagte than in almost any other battle. Their casualties were partly due to the high proportion of Europeans, who were much less ready than the Boers to flee when defeated. Dr Coster, a respected Dutch lawyer, was reported to have 'laid down his life because in a stupid moment Kruger had taunted him and his compatriots with cowardice'. Other distinguished foreigners killed included Count Zeppelin; and General Kock died of wounds later. The British casualties were 50 killed and 113 wounded. Hamilton's recommendation for the V.C. was rejected because it was feared that such personal bravery by a brigadier might set a dangerous precedent.

With two reverses in two successive days, the Transvaalers received a severe check, but White dissipated the fruits of Elandslaagte. Alarmed by reports that 10,000 Free Staters were advancing on Ladysmith, he precipitately withdrew all his forces into the town and the disorganized Transvaalers were not pursued, no bridges were destroyed and most of the stores round Elandslaagte were abandoned. Yule's force was ordered back from Dundee. After a circuitous four-day march in dreadful weather, they reached Ladysmith without loss or hindrance. To aid Yule a contingent from Ladysmith made a foray on 24 October, to fight a minor engagement with the Free Staters at Rietfontein.

Numbering about 23,500 men, the Transvaal and Orange Free State armies joined hands on 26 October, but did not yet fully invest Ladysmith. Bolstered up by the apparent successes at Talana and Elandslaagte, White felt confident of gaining a decisive victory, and he devised a vague, complicated and ambitious three-pronged attack. On 30 October almost all his formations were to march out of Ladysmith at night to take up their positions before dawn. The main attack was to be in two parts. First, a strong brigade under Colonel Grimwood was to seize Long Hill, an important feature about four miles north-east of the town, and then continue two miles to the north, joining Hamilton's brigade. This combined force was to assault the Boer stronghold at Pepworth Hill, the far side of the road and railway to Newcastle. Simultaneously, French's cavalry brigade was to occupy Lombard's Nek, about five miles east of Ladysmith. From there they were to protect Grimwood's right flank and, after the attack on Pepworth Hill, charge north to cut off the Boers who, it was anticipated, would retreat towards Newcastle. Finally, 1,140 men, under Colonel Carleton, were to march six miles north from Ladysmith, through the Boer

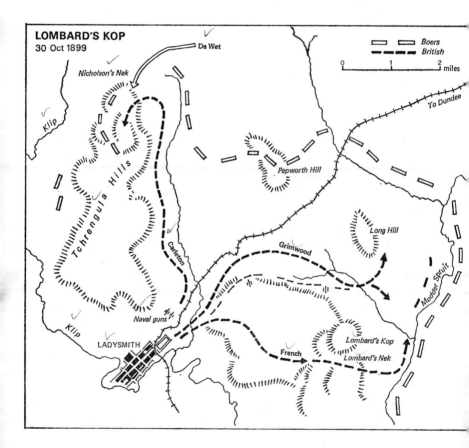

lines to seize the high ground of Nicholson's Nek. The purpose of this detached force was none too clear.

Predictably, almost nothing went according to plan. French's cavalry failed to reach Lombard's Nek, being held back two miles short of their objective. When daylight came Grimwood found no Boers on Long Hill but, owing to French's failure to obey orders, his right flank was in the air and well-directed Boer fire came from across the Modder Spruit where Louis Botha had taken over command. The infantry had continually to extend its front towards Lombard's Kop until some of the cavalry were encountered. Grimwood could obtain no directions from White who merely reinforced him. Meanwhile, highly mobile Boers were steadily enveloping the British who were mostly pinned down by small arms and artillery fire. After receiving an erroneous message from Ladysmith that Boer forces were going to attack the few troops left there, White decided to recall his troops. Once Grimwood's tired soldiers exposed themselves by moving into the open the encircling Boers poured fire on them, causing some to panic as they rushed for the safety of the town. Throughout the day Grimwood's artillery had been well deployed and shot with great accuracy. Finally, with little or no infantry protection, they brought their guns back with gallantry and calmness. Many Boer horsemen were itching to dash into the disorganized mass of troops, but Joubert refused, quoting a proverb, 'When God holds out a finger, don't take the whole hand'.

Delayed in starting, Carleton decided to occupy a nearer hill, at Tchrengula (Kainguba). As the troops began their ascent, the mules of the artillery battery stampeded, passing through the two infantry battalions. Recovering quickly, Carleton pressed on in the dark, but when he gained the summit, he concluded that the ground was too extensive to hold so he concentrated his force. Alerted by the noise, Boers under Christiaan de Wet crept up and exploited their sharp-shooting skill. A small party of the British being cut off, they hoisted a white handkerchief and, already short of ammunition, lacking water and exhausted by the heat, Carleton felt obliged to follow suit and surrendered the rest of the force. During the morning White heard from stragglers of Carleton's plight but could do nothing to extricate him.

For the British, the one bright spot this day was the arrival of five long-range naval guns, two 4·7 in. and three 12 pounders, which were rapidly brought into action and helped silence the Boer artillery during the withdrawal; the train which brought them in made its last journey out that afternoon, taking French and Colonel Haig. White refused to allow the cavalry, useless in a siege, to try to break out and reach the forces in Natal. For the Boers, the battle of Lombard's Kop was a memorable victory and the publicity attendant on nearly 1,000 British prisoners being marched through Pretoria provided a welcome boost for their morale and for recruiting in Cape Colony and abroad.

Although November, 1899, was an undramatic month, it was a most important period for both sides. By their efficient dispatch of troops and material, the British ensured that they would not lose the war, while the Boers, by immobilizing most of their forces in the sieges of Ladysmith, as well as of Kimberley and Mafeking, let slip their best chance of victory.

Rightly detested by most professional soldiers as wasting trained manpower and distorting proper strategic aims, sieges have always had a special appeal to the British public. Providing their own soldiers are being besieged, this slow-moving, intelligible form of warfare is felt to epitomize the dogged courage that the British people regard as most suited to their character (for example, Tobruk in 1941). Thus these three sieges galvanized British public opinion into seeing this war carried through to a victorious conclusion, irrespective of the cost. Against the resolute British defenders the ensuing siege warfare demanded a high degree of military discipline, as well as technical skills and specialized equipment, all of which the Boers lacked. Many of their senior commanders were also fearful of advancing any distance when this involved leaving in their rear professional troops whom they wrongly thought might try to break out to threaten their homelands. The Boer leaders never faced up to these problems, but drifted into a compromise fatal to their cause, and thus came to employ most of their troops in these three half-hearted sieges.

As the siege and relief of Ladysmith dominated much of the strategy of the war from November, 1899 to February, 1900, it will now be described, even though this means anticipating events a little. The British established themselves within an almost circular area whose perimeter measured about 14 miles, but their defences suffered from being overlooked by an outer ring of hills. Of the 21,300 people besieged, the garrison consisted of 13,500 soldiers having 51 guns, with only about 300 rounds each. The town was stocked with rations for at least eight weeks' normal consumption, while the Klip River provided a constant, but polluted, water supply. As is usual in a long siege, the most potent threat was disease, but White was incredibly fortunate because the humane Joubert, to the anger of many of his subordinates, sanctioned the establishment of a hospital camp outside the perimeter. There the sick, wounded and any non-combatants who desired were sent during an armistice on 5 November; and thenceforward a daily train was allowed to bring in the sick and wounded who eventually numbered 1,500. The garrison was thus spared the demoralizing physical and psychological burden of caring for their most critically sick whose numbers increased continuously; of 810 who died, over 500 succumbed to disease.

The siege soon developed into a haphazard affair. Leader of the Irish Brigade, the self-styled Colonel Blake, was an American Uitlander who had been trained as a cavalry officer at West Point. His account of the proceedings seems fairly realistic: 'When it was sufficiently light to see moving objects in and about Ladysmith, all the Long Toms and howitzers would open up and drive every one into the hole provided for safety. After that silence could reign until

about ten a.m., when an artillery duel would be fought . . .
Then all would be quiet again until after 4 p.m. Not a day
passed without a set-to taking place between one or more of
the commandos and the English. If the latter did not come
out, the Boers would go in, and, in many instances some very
hot skirmishes resulted . . . the Boers had a delightful time,
lived in luxury, had their sports, smoked their pipes, drank
their coffee, entertained visiting friends and when there was a
fight they were always ready for it.' Reitz recalled, 'During
the daytime no guards were set at all, as there was always a
sufficient number of men on the hill above amusing themselves with sniping to make sure of alarm being given in case
of need, and at night . . . we went on outpost so close to the
English sentries that we would hear them challenge each
other, and sometimes exchanged shouted pleasantries with
them.' A more dedicated soldier, Villebois-Mareuil, was
shocked by what he saw before leaving in disgust for
Kimberley. He blamed Joubert whom he castigated as
'essentially a politician who knows nothing about war and
may continue to vegetate around Ladysmith'. He added,
'Headquarters' staff is composed of relatives of General
Joubert, Mr Malan, his son-in-law, carrying out the duties of
Chief of the Staff, whilst Mrs Joubert may be compared to
Quartermaster-General. They are all very friendly and easy
of access, with the exception of Mrs Joubert. As a whole,
headquarters, with its animals, negresses, and large tents, is
more fair-like than military.'

At first the Boers had naïvely expected that the shelling
by their seven heavy guns would compel the garrison to
capitulate, but it soon became obvious that these were making
little impression on troops and positions scattered over so
large an area. Joubert was, however, content with trying
slowly to starve the garrison into submission. The siege
was only punctuated by two outbursts of military activity.
Just before the forthcoming Battle of Colenso, White
authorized two successful night sorties against the large Boer
guns, but felt that the loss of 20 killed and over 40 wounded

and missing on the second occasion was too heavy a price to pay and these forays were discontinued. The second major event was an attack which the Government and a War Council forced Joubert to make. It was directed against the Platrand, the most southerly and detached of the British positions. These fortifications were scattered along a ridge 600 feet high, 800–1,000 yards broad and two and a half miles long; its eastern end was known as Caesar's Camp and its western as Wagon Hill. Ian Hamilton commanded the composite force of about 1,000 British troops who garrisoned it. On the night of 5–6 January the Boers planned that 600 Free Staters should storm Wagon Hill, while 900 Trans-vaalers would attack the more strongly held Caesar's Camp and be supported by a further 500 troops if the need arose. A diversionary thrust was also to be mounted against Observation Hill, an important British outpost at the northern extremity of the perimeter. Many of those chosen funked the operation but those who persevered and clambered up the steep slopes failed to surprise the defenders, and only a few groups of Boers gained footholds. Soon after dawn the Transvaalers were driven off the heights of Caesar's Camp by shrapnel fire, but despite some hand-to-hand fighting it took powerful British reinforcements the whole day to dislodge the Free Staters on Wagon Hill. The majority of Boer commandos took no part in the battle, and the sporadic artillery fire against Observation Hill caused White little anxiety. 225 British were killed and probably over 100 Boers but these losses led to the Boers reverting to the less expensive policy of trying to starve the garrison into surrender.

Perhaps the greatest waste of Boer manpower was Piet Cronje's force of over 6,000 (nearly 15% of their troops) who, from 13 October, besieged Mafeking. Its garrison was a mere 1,200 combatants, plus 300 white women, 400 children and an embarrassing 7,500 natives who refused to leave. For the Boers the town had a symbolic value dis-proportionate to its size and negligible strategic importance because it was situated so close to their border and was on the railway; furthermore, it was from here that Dr Jameson had launched his Raid. (He had tried to return, but Baden-Powell refused to have him.) For weeks before the war, Baden-Powell had been stocking the town with supplies and preparing it for attack by building shell-proof shelters and laying minefields, whose extent he purposely exaggerated. The publicity given to this 217-day siege was due to three main reasons. First the personality of Baden-Powell whose amusing communiques were a refreshing change from the normal pattern; for instance: 'October 21. All well. Four hours bombardment. One dog killed.' Secondly, locked up in Mafeking were several well-connected people, including the Prime Minister's son, Major Lord Edward Cecil and two earls' sons. The Duke of Marlborough's daughter, Lady Sarah Wilson, managed, early in December, to rejoin her husband who was on Baden-Powell's Staff. Finally, the newspaper world was strongly represented with correspondents from *The Times*, the *Pall Mall Gazette*, the *Daily Chronicle* and *Morning Post*. Most of the desultory fighting occurred before the end of October. After two small attacks, Cronje realized that to take Mafeking against such determined resistance would be too costly and he began the futile process of bombarding it with a Long Tom gun, nicknamed Creaky, and trying to starve the garrison into surrender. The siege became farcical with Baden-Powell and the Boers often exchanging notes under flags of truce. Sunday was strictly observed by the Boers as a day of rest, enabling the defenders to emerge to enjoy picnics and to exercise themselves; until the Boers objected, even games of polo were played. Regular communications with the outside world were maintained by native runners who slipped through the lines to the nearest friendly telegraph office about 50 miles to the north. In the middle of November, Cronje departed with 4,000 men and most of the guns and Snyman took over the apathetic besiegers.

With 50,000 inhabitants (18,000 of whom were white

men), the diamond town of Kimberley was much larger than either Ladysmith or Mafeking. It lies over 50 miles north of the Orange River and, being so far out on a limb (it is west and slightly north of Bloemfontein), its defence caused the British great concern. At the end of September, less than 600 soldiers had been sent there under Colonel Kekwich to try to prepare the place for a siege. Immediately before the war, Rhodes himself went to Kimberley, perhaps to act as a potential hostage for the town's security, since the Boers had threatened to parade him through the streets of Pretoria in a cage if he fell into their hands. He took a keen interest in its defence and Major Taylor of the Royal Artillery wrote, 'I dined with Mr Rhodes one evening and he asked me what I wanted . . . Within three days he sent me 74 horses, 92 mules, harness and saddlery complete, seven large buck wagons and six carts'. On the outbreak of war, Kekwich had less than 1,000 trained troops, including some Cape Police. His forces grew to about 4,800, the large volunteer element consisting of de Beers' employees who owed their livelihood and their loyalty to Rhodes, a situation that was to create friction between him and Kekwich. Early in November, Wessels, leader of the Boer forces, had assembled 7,500 men. He sent a formal demand of surrender that was rejected and the half-hearted siege began. Being well provisioned, the town was in little danger, but to safeguard the water supply a detachment had to be placed at the Premier Mine, just outside the 14-mile defensive perimeter. With hindsight, it is evident that the investing Boer forces were not a serious threat, but at the time Milner and other British leaders were genuinely and understandably alarmed. The fall of Ladysmith or Kimberley, or both, could have precipitated a possibly fatal crisis of confidence within Cape Colony, where the large Afrikaans population was only waiting for a definite Boer victory before rising against British rule.

Besides immobilizing about 35,000 men in these three sieges, the Boers further dissipated their forces by splitting them into three groups. In the north, about 2,000 men were detached to protect 750 miles of border against Plumer who, in Bechuanaland and Rhodesia, had only about 1,600 locally recruited soldiers and police. A proposal that, having crossed the Limpopo into Rhodesia, Boer troops should march on Bulawayo, was rejected and, later in November, this force was withdrawn, permitting Plumer to make a successful sortie into Transvaal in December.

South of Mafeking, de la Rey was far more active. Annexing Vryburg, he crossed the border with 7,500 men and, virtually unopposed, took most of Southern Bechuanaland. Except for Kimberley and its immediate environs the Boers therefore held both sides of the railway line from north of Mafeking down almost to Orange River Station in Cape Colony.

A third group, about 4,500 strong, was spread along the Orange River border with Cape Colony. Early in November some of these Free Staters crossed the Orange, seizing the railway bridges at Norval's Pont and Bethulie, and then advanced very slowly into the adjoining district of Cape Colony, finding many supporters. This invasion seriously threatened the two important railway junctions at de Aar and Naauwpoort, where large quantities of stores had been unloaded, but the Boers here were ill-led and made no further moves.

At the beginning of November, the British were in an unenviable situation. Nearly half their forces were locked up in Ladysmith, Kimberley and Mafeking, while their remaining troops were outnumbered and spread thinly over hundreds of miles of frontier. Thus they sorely needed a lull in the fighting, and this soon occurred, for as now became evident, the Boers had no real strategic plan for waging the war. Not only did they fail to appreciate that they must exploit their favourable position quickly if they were to win, but they also could not bring themselves to appoint a supreme commander with authority to coordinate the activities of their citizen armies, who were unwilling to risk quitting their homelands to invade Cape Colony and Natal.

Furthermore the Boers' advantage was of a very transitory nature because they could not expect any significant increase in their military strength, whereas substantial British reinforcements were due to arrive during November and December.

The Army Sea Transport was responsible for the dispatch overseas of troops and stores. Founded in 1876, this little-known joint naval-military organization had to overcome some formidable problems. Its small staff had rapidly to charter dozens of vessels, many of which needed adapting, this being especially the case for those transporting the cavalry and artillery regiments whose men could not be separated from their horses. As it was most unusual for large numbers of men and animals to travel together for over three weeks, these ships had often to be fitted with extra decks, the men always having to be accommodated on wooden decks and, for various technical reasons, be carried below the horses. Horses also could not be kept on metal decks, nor, because of the extreme climatic variations, could they be stalled on the open upper deck which was anyhow required for exercising the soldiers. The pressure on the Army Sea Transport reached its peak between 20 October and 30 November when 58,000 men, 9,000 horses and large quantities of stores were safely sent on the 6,000 miles voyage from England to Cape Town. Thanks to the huge British merchant shipping fleet and the efficiency of the Army Sea Transport, the necessities of war always flowed smoothly into South Africa.

Although the mobilization and dispatch of the 46,000 strong Army Corps was expertly handled, it was an unimpressive fighting force, suffering, among other things, from many shortages of equipment. For example, the reserve uniforms were still of the old red or blue colours, and even the new khaki drill was too thin and had to be replaced by serge; home-pattern boots were useless for South Africa as the uppers came apart from the soles and hand-sewn boots had to be issued; the quantities of harness and saddlery held were totally inadequate, while the number of carts was far below requirements and they were unsuitable for South African conditions; all the pontoons in store could not span a river 100 yards wide; finally no reserve hospital equipment had ever been bought. These deficiencies can be blamed partly on the perennial meanness of the Treasury, partly on the lethargy of successive War Ministers and partly on the incompetence of the senior civilians and soldiers in the War Office. But the newly appointed and very able Director-General of Ordnance, General Sir Henry Brackenbury, remedied these shortages sufficiently quickly to prevent them endangering the early operations.

Once in action, other and more fundamental defects soon emerged, particularly the low technical military standards of many officers and men and their poor education, the stupidity of some of the Commanders, and the lack of a proper intelligence system. Perhaps the most glaring weakness was the obsolete training. Fuller recollected a system that looked 'upon war as an unending succession of Peninsula engagements . . . It never considered what the enemy might or might not do . . . It was rigidly formal, rigidly conventional and rigidly exact. To doubt the doctrine of the 1896 Drill Book, with its columns and its echelons and its squares, would have been heretical . . . When this is realized, I feel we ought to be charitably disposed towards those gallant gentlemen who led us from one tactical absurdity into another; for they had been schooled in a system which was absurdity itself.'

Three closely connected points must be made about the nature of the Army Corps. First, to call it a corps is a misnomer; rather it was an expeditionary force composed of individual units that, except in the case of one of its six infantry brigades, had never trained together. The Army Corps was therefore an ad hoc body, bearing little resemblance to the military corps as known in the continental, and later in British armies. Secondly neither the Corps Headquarters itself nor the four divisional headquarters possessed staffs trained to plan and co-ordinate the movement of the troops under their nominal control. Even if such professionally trained staff officers had been available, it is doubtful whether the senior commanders would have known how to employ them; when his Chief-of-Staff, Hunter, was locked up in Ladysmith, Buller never replaced him. Later Roberts misused Kitchener, and Rawlinson, who was on Roberts' staff in 1900, complained that 'all departments of headquarters wire (to Cape Town) in the name of the Chief-of-Staff, usually without consulting each other and each claims precedence for its own requirements. Kitchener, nominally Chief-of-Staff, is nearly always away doing odd jobs where things are going wrong and there is no one here to pull the machinery together for Roberts.' Kitchener dispensed with a Chief-of-Staff for about nine months, and when Ian Hamilton was appointed, his duties were much the same as those Roberts had given to Kitchener. Finally, nearly all the senior officers were moulded by a school of thought which made it virtually inconceivable for them to decentralize their authority, even if the machinery had existed. They regarded this war as merely a larger kind of colonial punitive expedition in which they were column commanders who had to 'run the show'. They therefore planned their battles, drafted the orders for them and, as far as possible, personally supervised the detailed conduct of the fighting. Roberts tried to run the advance on Pretoria in much the same way as he had organized his famous march to Khandahar in 1880.

In addition to the shortcomings in equipment, training and organization, the Army Corps was handicapped by the unfortunate choice of Buller. Admittedly, he had half-heartedly told Lansdowne in June that he did not feel competent to be the commander-in-chief of the expeditionary force, never having exercised independent command. But he permitted himself to be overruled, largely because there was no convincing substitute; Wolseley and Roberts, both at 66, were considered too old, and Kitchener, then in Egypt, too young. Moreover, Buller seemed to possess, in an embarrassing degree, all the qualities of a great general. Exceedingly brave, with a long, varied and generally successful military career, including service in South Africa, at 60 he was neither too old nor too young. He cared for his soldiers' welfare and they adored him. His bulky figure, his imposing, if somewhat brusque and forbidding, manner, his wealth, his happy marriage and finally his outward appearance of self-confidence, all made Buller the obvious choice to lead the elite troops of the British Army to a quick and dashing victory over what was thought to be a rabble of backwoodsmen with no military expertise. Most informed opinion in Britain expected the war would be over by Christmas. But the real Buller bore little resemblance to the public image. He may have been undergoing the male change of life, or it may have been the cumulative effects of an intensely active life combined with unstinted good living, but whatever the causes, his energy was soon exhausted. Even in 1895, Brigadier (later General Sir Neville) Lyttelton had noted, 'I took part in a Staff Ride in Sussex under Buller's supervision and was much taken by surprise at his want of push and enterprise.' Buller's solicitude for his men made him too easily downcast by casualties, inevitable if a stubborn enemy is to be defeated. As a result, he suffered from bouts of depression and lacked that inner self-confidence and resolution so necessary, not only for devising and carrying through a plan of attack, but also for surmounting the setbacks and rebuffs attendant upon a battle. He once admitted, 'I was better as a second-in-command in a complex military affair than as an officer in chief command.' Finally he lacked that indefinable quality, essential in a great commander, which the French term *coup d'oeil militaire*; he could not quickly pick out the vital features in the ground over which he had to fight and then put them into their proper perspective when drawing up his plans.

Soon after disembarking on 31 October, Buller decided to split the Army Corps. Although later censured for this step, contemporary opinion supported him, contending that, for political and military reasons, the most pressing needs were to protect Natal and relieve Ladysmith. To this theatre of the war, Buller dispatched Clery, Commander of 2 Division, with a considerable proportion of the artillery and some of the cavalry. In Cape Colony, Buller divided the troops into three unequal parts. The largest force was placed under Lord Methuen, who was ordered to relieve Kimberley as soon as possible. Recalled from Natal, French took most of the cavalry division to guard the Colesberg area and protect the important railway links at de Aar and Naauw-poort. Finally, Gatacre, divested of nearly all his troops in 3 Division, was given a collection of units both to try to stem any Boer advances from Stormberg and to control as much as possible of the turbulent north-eastern corner of Cape Colony. Also additional mounted troops were locally recruited, mostly commanded by Regular British soldiers like Thorneycroft in Natal and Brabant in Cape Colony. The only sizeable staff was in the Corps Headquarters which Buller transferred to Forestier-Walker at Cape Town, who, although in charge of the lines of communication and administration, had no staff of his own—a curious oversight. These arrangements were made during the first half of November and when most of the units of the Army Corps disembarked during the latter half of that month, they were expeditiously posted. Simultaneously, it was agreed that another division would be sent from England. Furthermore, 2,500 Colonial volunteers were accepted and some Australians arrived at the end of November; many more were clamouring to serve, but the home government was apprehensive of accepting them, fearing that their pay of 5/– per day, as opposed to the British soldiers' 1/–, might lead to trouble. Foolishly, the War Office emphasized that infantry units were preferable to cavalry.

These new dispositions inevitably led to the postponement of the original plan of a rapid advance up the centre of Orange Free State to occupy Bloemfontein. Buller's subsequent performance in this campaign must cast the gravest doubts on whether he was capable of leading a swift offensive action anywhere. Discounting this so-far-unknown factor, as well as ignoring the Boer threats, the many problems of organization and acclimatization still precluded any speedy invasion. Nevertheless, such was his ill-founded optimism that, on 6 November, Buller forecast that this central thrust could start in January. He assumed Kimberley and Ladysmith would be quickly relieved allowing the necessary redeployment.

Buller's measures had so far been based on a sound judgement and appreciation of what it was reasonable to do in difficult circumstances that were none of his making. On 22 November he made his first major blunder by suddenly leaving for Natal. By shifting from Cape Town, where he left nearly all his staff, he could no longer act as commander-in-chief and ran the risk of interfering in the Natal campaign over which Clery had been given command.

CHAPTER FOUR

The Relief Columns

' "It seems to me", said a well-known colonel of the Guards, "that our leaders find out the strongest position of the enemy, and then attack him in front".
' "It appears to me", put in a brother officer, "that they attack him first, and find out his position afterwards".'

> *E. Kinnear*, To the Modder River with Methuen,
> *1900.*

'One read in the papers that the bad reconnoitring by the English baffled description, and their general training was condemned on those grounds. As an eye-witness I must protest against these attacks on the English army. The reconnoitring patrols which were sent out had to examine many square miles of barren country and spy the enemy. This country could not be reconnoitred by a few men.'

> *From Count Sternberg's*
> My Experiences of the Boer War, *1900.*

On 21 November Methuen opened the British offensive, setting out from Orange River Station to relieve Kimberley, 75 miles up the line. 10,000 strong, his division consisted of two infantry brigades, the Guards and 9th, twelve 15 pounder guns, four naval 12 pounder guns with a Blue-Jackets detachment, four companies of Royal Engineers, some Medical Corps, but only about 850 cavalry or mounted infantry. Methuen was well aware that his force suffered from severe handicaps. The shortage of cavalry would make reconnaissance difficult and prevent any wide flanking move-ments around the natural obstacles that lay across the railway along which, for logistic reasons, he had to advance. Having only just disembarked three of the four Guards regiments less than a week beforehand, and having come up by train from Cape Town at once, nearly the distance from London to Berlin, neither the men nor the horses were acclimatized to the extremes of the summer heat and cold on the veld, over 1,250 metres up. The troops were unaccustomed to judging distances, most deceptive in the very clear air, they were unaware of the many deposits of ironstones which affected compasses and they had no reliable maps. Movements could not be kept secret; Allenby wrote of this district, 'Although we are still in Cape Colony, we are practically in a hostile country, as nearly all the farmers are disloyal and most of them have already left their farms and joined the Boers; while those who remain act as spies'. Methuen took many sensible precautions: tents were left behind and the minimum of kit was allowed; to help concealment all bright metal objects, like buttons, were painted khaki (An outraged sergeant wrote, 'I believe that they will be making us dye our whiskers khaki colour next'.); to conserve water, shaving was forbidden and to blur the distinction between officers and men, both dressed alike; Methuen described himself as looking 'like a second-class conductor in a khaki coat with no mark of rank on it and a Boer hat and in Norwegian slippers'.

Between 21 and 25 November Methuen fought two minor but successful engagements, the first, on 23 November, at Belmont, about 16 miles north of the Orange River. Stretching three miles to the south-east of this small railway station, an outcrop of rocky hills rises sharply 50–100 metres above the featureless plain. Here Jacobus Prinsloo had assembled 2,000 men, two guns and a pom-pom to try to bar the British advance. As long as the Boers retained this stronghold, they dominated the railway, the British life-line. Close reconnaissance was impossible and Methuen based his plan on a hurriedly drawn and inaccurate sketch map. He decided on the conventional night approach march, followed by a dawn attack with covering artillery fire. Methuen insisted that the infantry should advance in extended order, to minimize the effect of Boer rifle fire. The assault was late in starting, surprise was lost, and some units, being partly misled by the map, found themselves in the wrong position, but despite these and other mistakes, the two brigades reacted quickly to perform their allotted roles. Once the British troops began to climb up the kopjes and threaten the Boers with bayonets, most of them fled. The British lost about 75 killed and 220 wounded; the Boers had about 100 casualties and 50 were taken prisoner.

Ten miles further on, between Graspan and Enslin, is another small range of hills. An attempted reconnaissance was driven off, but on 24 November it was reported that this strong position athwart the railway was only lightly held by de la Rey with about 400 men and two guns; but during that afternoon Prinsloo reinforced him with nearly 200 Free Staters. Methuen only discovered this early on 25 November when an artillery duel revealed that the Boers had occupied most of the hills. His original plan, to bombard the Boer lines and attack frontally along the railway, had to be scrapped and he hurriedly switched the main thrust to the south-eastern corner of this cluster of kopjes. One of Rimington's Scouts described the scene: 'A wide plain . . . flat as the sea and all along the farther side a line of kopjes and hills rising like reefs and detached islands out of it. You might think that the plain was empty at first glance, but if you look hard you will see . . . little khaki-clad figures dotted all over it . . . along the sides of those hills, puffs of white smoke float out . . . The artillery duel goes on between the two, while still the infantry, unmolested as yet, crawls and crawls towards those hills.'

Not engaged at Belmont, the 250-strong Naval Brigade led the attack with the utmost valour. But they lost nearly half their strength, because their officers would not dress like their men, and because they bunched up too closely, thereby presenting the Boer riflemen with excellent targets. The well-dispersed supporting infantry suffered few losses.

Nevertheless, the surviving sailors and Marines, and the North Lancashire Regiment, carried on and, as more and more troops clambered up the kopje, the Boers again turned and fled. As at Belmont, the cavalry were too weak to molest their retreat. By 10.00 hours the affair was over. All the three British officers and six out of the 15 men killed were from the Naval Brigade, as were 92/143 of the wounded. The Boers probably lost 50 killed and wounded and 40 prisoners.

The next obstacle was the Modder River, on reaching which Methuen would have completed 54 of the 75 miles to Kimberley. On 23 November, from the besieged town, Major Taylor began a cheerful letter to his mother, 'I climb up to the top of our Conning Tower which is in the centre of the Town, and where Colonel Kekwich and myself run the show from. He gives me a free hand to work at the Artillery . . . and is a charming man to serve under'. He commented on the Boers' shells: 'They contained very small bursting charges (and there was no velocity in the shell itself), they simply opened out under ground . . . Any lucky person who could find all the pieces of a shell and fit them together generally got £10 . . . Our only losses from the bombardment was one old Kaffir woman! We have had several men killed and wounded in sorties from Kimberley . . . We hope to be relieved in 3 or 4 more days.'

The fact that Kimberley was not relieved for another twelve and a half weeks was largely due to the untutored military genius of 'Koos' de la Rey. This 50-year-old farmer, who resembled an Old Testament prophet, had seen the tactical error of trying to hold rocky fortresses, as at Belmont and Graspan, where the Boer riflemen had to fire downwards, resulting in 'plunging' fire which is always wasteful. He realized that once the attackers reached the base of the kopjes, they were in 'dead' ground which gave them the opportunity to regroup before beginning the ascent, when quite good cover was available. De la Rey's remedy was for the Boers to adopt new and revolutionary tactics. Instead of sitting perched up above the ground in natural fortresses,

5 'Roughing it'. The Officers Mess of the Grenadier Guards at Modder.

6 Wounded soldiers in a wagon house at Klip Drift on the Modder, February, 1900.

7   Bullock teams crossing the Modder at Koodoes Rand Drift after Paardeberg. The remains of the Boer laager can be seen on the left.

8   The dug-outs at Paardeberg where British prisoners were kept.

they should dig into the earth to conceal themselves. Thereby, they would gain the maximum effect from their rifle fire which, by being directed level with and close to the ground ('grazing' fire), would be lethal for all the 2,200 yards of its trajectory, as opposed to the downward-aimed fire from the high ground that plunged straight into the ground.

Besides having to convince the Boer commanders of the soundness of his proposals, de la Rey, still a relatively minor general, had to coerce the despondent Free Staters into making yet another stand. On the eve of the Modder River battle he received considerable support from Cronje, who had arrived from Mafeking on 27 November with 1,200 Transvaalers. It was agreed that the Boer forces would try to hold the southern bank of the river lines on either side of the road-ferry and rail bridge. This position was wonderfully suited for proving the soundness of de la Rey's theories, because the ground possessed many features favouring the kind of defensive tactics he envisaged. Like most of the rivers in South Africa, both the Riet and the Modder flow through cuttings scoured out of the soft earth to a depth of about 30 feet. The river bed itself is about 30 feet across, but the shallow valley through which it runs varies from 100–200 yards in width. With their gently sloping banks, these rivers lie concealed, with only the tops of bushes, usually mimosa, sometimes marking their paths like a low hedgerow. Unfordable except in very few places, both the Modder and the Riet follow very tortuous courses. Although the general direction of their flow is from east to west, the Modder makes a large loop just upstream from their junction, while the Riet almost meets the Modder before it swings southwards for about three miles, to run nearly parallel with the road and railway along which Methuen approached the crossing places.

De la Rey placed most of his 3,500 soldiers along the southern bank of the Riet on either side of the village of Rosmead; this western part of the line was held by Prinsloo's Free Staters, some of whom had actually been

3

persuaded to fight with the river behind them. De la Rey's own commando, the Lichtenburg, was in the centre, protecting the road-ferry and rail bridge. In the eastern and longest sector, the Transvaalers dug themselves in just below the lip of the valley where, well concealed by bushes, they had an uninterrupted field of fire over flat open ground; in this eastern flank, all the three pom-poms were far forward. Four of the six guns were concentrated in the centre, behind the river and near the road and railway, the other two supported the Transvaalers. The position was further strengthened by the excellent covered lateral communications afforded by the river valleys along which, if needs be, troops could be switched to reinforce any part of the line. These dispositions suffered from one serious weakness, both flanks were left 'in the air' and could be turned easily by a superior force; but de la Rey assumed that Methuen would make a frontal attack into what was, to all intents and purposes, a huge ambush, and he obligingly did so.

Having dislodged the Boers from Belmont and Graspan within a week, the British continued their advance in a confident mood. Rightly, Methuen was anxious to keep the Boers on the run and, on 27 November, 1st Division pushed on 14 miles. Under 20 miles away, the Kimberley garrison could now signal by searchlight and their messages indicated that the Boers were hoping to make a final stand at the Spytfontein ridge, about a dozen miles south of the town. Methuen decided to outflank this position by marching east to the town of Jacobsdal, turning north on to the main Kimberley road and crossing the Modder at Brown's Drift. He then meant to assemble his forces at Abon's Dam before attacking the Boers, whom he assumed to be at Spytfontein, from the flank. This risky 30-mile advance involved carrying five days supplies, but Methuen hoped to pick up more at Jacobsdal, the depot of the Orange Free State Army. Methuen expected the Boers to retain only a token force at the Modder bridge which he proposed to mask with 1,000 troops and the four naval guns. With no proper maps, he relied largely on a hurried sketch by O'Meara, which was inaccurate in several respects, suggesting that the rivers were fordable almost everywhere. Although very short of horsed troops, Methuen blundered, first by not trying to reconnoitre the country over which he proposed to move; and secondly by disregarding earlier cavalry warnings that the Modder bridge area was being reinforced. Moreover, he wrongly interpreted the westward movement of the Transvaalers, which he observed personally, believing their move to be directed towards Spytfontein.

Very early on 28 November, authoritative reports reached British headquarters which left no doubt that the Boers were deployed in strength around the Modder bridge. Fearing for his flank and lines of communication, Methuen felt compelled to abandon his original plan and hurriedly instructed 1st Division to march straight at the bridge, with Colvile's Guards Brigade to the east of and Pole-Carew's 9th Brigade mainly to the west of the road and railway. Orders were only issued at 04.30 and few soldiers had more than time for a cup of tea before they started their march at 05.00 hours. At first all went smoothly, and Cronje became alarmed because the 9th Lancers, on the east flank, appeared to be going to seize Bosman's Drift across the Riet. Had they realized its existence, the British could have easily out-flanked the Boer positions. But Cronje hurriedly directed a gun and a pom-pom forward to shell the cavalry who, with no orders to try to cross the Riet, spent the rest of the day there being sniped at.

Meanwhile, the infantry advanced steadily on a wide front of about three miles and by 08.00 hours were less than a mile from the river. So far there were no signs of life and nobody took any notice of the whitewashed stones dotted about as range markers for the Boer riflemen and the artillery. Methuen was well forward and chose a house the other side of the river for his new headquarters. Colvile recalled, ' "They'll never stand against us here" was said more than once in my hearing . . . As we watched Arthur

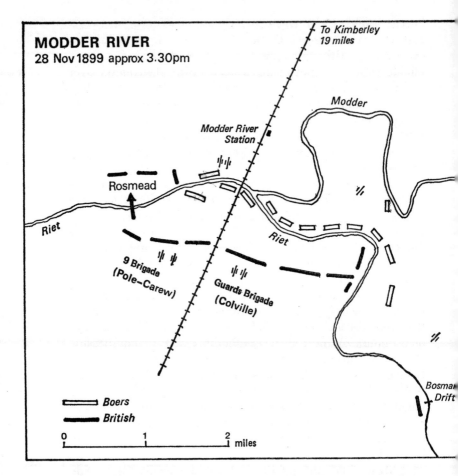

MODDER RIVER
28 Nov 1899 approx 3.30pm

To Kimberley
19 miles

Modder

Modder River
Station

Rosmead

Riet

Riet

9 Brigade
(Pole-Carew)

Guards Brigade
(Colville)

Bosman
Drift

☐☐☐ Boers
▬▬▬ British

0   1   2 miles

Paget and his Scots Guards moving ahead to the right, Lord
Methuen said to me, "They are not here". "They are sitting
uncommonly tight if they are, sir!" I answered; and, as if
they had heard him, the Boers answered too with a roar of
musketry.'

Using smokeless powder in their rifles, this fire came
from unseen troops about 1,200 yards away. It would have
been devastating if the Boers had only waited until the

British were 500 yards distant. Although causing few casualties, the fusillade immediately pinned the British down and their attempts to dash forward all failed. Amid the low scrub and anthills the three Guards regiments were safe as long as they lay flat. Directly they raised themselves up to retaliate, Boer riflemen and pom-poms opened up, and no amount of shelling by the British artillery could dislodge the Boers from their trenches. Hoping to work round the flank, Colvile ordered his reserve batallion to prolong the line to the east, but the soldiers found themselves unexpectedly hemmed in by the Riet. Finding no ford, they failed to get behind the Boers and had to dig themselves into the river bank. Soon after 09.00 hours, therefore, Methuen's eastern flank was immobilized for the remainder of the battle, the Guardsmen suffering from the scorching heat (110°), from thirst and angry ants whose nests were disturbed.

On the western flank much the same thing happened and Pole-Carew's men were met by heavy rifle fire as they approached the river. Until soon after midday, therefore, a line of prone Guardsmen stretched from the Riet to the railway, while, for over a mile westward, nearly four battalions of the 9th Brigade were similarly pinned to the ground. But during the advance the Guards had veered so much to the west that almost none, as opposed to the planned half, of the 9th Brigade found itself east of the railway. This enabled Pole-Carew to extend his troops farther west than had been anticipated and he exploited the more favourable terrain on this flank. Appreciating that a detached farm-house probably held the key to his sector, he made his way there, where he joined the four companies of the Argyll and Sutherland Highlanders, whom he ordered to charge down to the river, which they did successfully. About 13.00 hours Methuen appeared, approved Pole-Carew's initiative and then personally led another group down to the river and returned unharmed. The Highlanders were now between the Boers on the north bank and those further upstream on the other side, so that the Free Staters could not fire without risking hitting their comrades in the farm-house area. Pole-Carew ordered another attack against the Boers in and around the farm, sensing correctly that they must be alarmed as their escape route was threatened. These Boers retreated to the north bank and, as they fled, they were joined by most of the Free Staters in Rosmead who had become demoralized by the sustained shelling.

Thus by 14.00 hours the Boers' western flank had collapsed and a complete British victory looked likely, but this was not to be. The main reason was a lack of reserves, nearly all of whom had been committed, depriving Pole-Carew of reinforcements; and with the Boers continuing to paralyse most of the British, it was impossible to disengage and transfer units. Nevertheless at about 15.00 hours, Pole-Carew mustered about 400 soldiers and tried to advance from Rosmead towards the Boer centre at the Modder River Station. He was soon halted, mainly by de la Rey's Transvaalers and by the fire from the three Free Stater guns whose crews, under the German, Albrecht, displayed great bravery despite heavy casualties. Pole-Carew now came under steady fire from his own artillery with whom he had no means of communicating, except by the rudimentary paraphernalia of flags and, when sunny and free from the smoke of battle, by heliograph. Certainly the naval guns, well in the rear, and probably the field guns deployed just behind the infantry, had not yet been informed of Pole-Carew's movements which were invisible to them. Thus they continued shelling the Boer gun positions, and other likely centres of resistance across the river, providing invaluable support. Two field batteries fired over 1,000 rounds each. Another battery covered 62 miles in 28 hours to reach the fighting; four of its horses died and 40 never recovered from this forced march, but these gunners fired 240 rounds before exhausting their ammunition.

To return to Pole-Carew; at 16.00 hours he was preparing another attack when he heard that Methuen had been wounded. Continually rushing up to the most forward positions, Methuen had exerted little grip over the direction of his hastily conceived plans, but at this crucial moment even this semblance of control ceased. Appointed to command, Colvile knew little of events on the other flank and decided to rush the Boers' trenches on his right after dark, using troops withdrawn under cover of an artillery bombardment. To soften up the Boer positions, he now ordered the guns to shell the whole front. Warned of this, Pole-Carew cancelled his plans, as Colvile did later, but without informing Pole-Carew. Although a fresh regiment had arrived, no attempt was made to enlarge the foothold on the north bank.

Early that night the Boers held a stormy council of war. Although his son had been mortally wounded, and despite the flight of nearly all the Free Staters, de la Rey still advocated holding on, but Cronje and the other leaders refused. So precipitate was their unnecessary withdrawal that the Boers left behind their guns; under the noses of the British, Albrecht and de la Rey returned later to collect them.

On 28 November Kekwich had sent out a sortie from Kimberley to the south and west, hoping to draw off troops from Methuen. Although employing nearly half his garrison, the 1,850 men achieved almost nothing and retreated that evening with the loss of 24 killed, including Colonel Scott Turner, the reckless leader of one of the columns. On 30 November, Taylor continued his letter in an optimistic vein, 'We hope to find the Relief force here soon, but they are 5 days over-due now'.

On 29 November 1st Division soon discovered that the Boers had retreated. For the loss of 71 dead and over 400 wounded and missing (5% of their force), the British had surmounted another obstacle on their path to Kimberley; the Boer losses were about 50 killed and probably 100 wounded. Methuen, not seriously wounded, paused till 11 December to rest his weary force and to repair the railway bridge over the Modder whose contaminated water was eagerly drunk; then, and even more after Paardeberg, 'Château Modder' acquired a well-earned but ghoulish reputation for being 'full of body';

the typhoid, cholera and dysentery germs which its corpse-laden waters bred killed and incapacitated more British soldiers in the next three months than the Boers did during the whole war.

To return briefly to the other front. Early in November, before most of the Army Corps began disembarking at Durban, the fate of Natal hung in the balance. Over 20,000 Boer troops around Ladysmith seemed poised for an invasion led by Joubert. On 3 November the British managed to assemble a scratch force of about 2,300 (less than 300 of them mounted) at Estcourt, but these troops were soon withdrawn to Frere. Forty-two miles back down the railway the larger town of Pietermaritzburg was almost defenceless. Seventy miles beyond it lay the vital port of Durban, but here the Navy had removed 28 guns from warships and positioned them on the outskirts of the town. Nevertheless, with so little to oppose them, the well-mounted Boer Commandos appeared to the British in Natal as a force whose progress could not be checked. In the Boer camp, however, opinions were deeply divided. An influential section considered it too risky merely to mask Ladysmith and advance to the coast, when this meant leaving 12,000 British Regular troops, not only across their lines of communication, but also between their main force and their homes. Joubert supported this cautious view, but, on 14 November, he agreed to a compromise whereby Botha took less than 4,000 mounted troops and five guns across the Tugela to push towards Pietermaritzburg; probably to restrain Botha, Joubert accompanied the expedition. The Boers had, however, delayed their start for too long. The Army Corps were beginning to land at Durban, although these reinforcements did not prevent the British from conducting a remarkably half-hearted campaign.

One of the more ludicrous episodes involved a reconnaissance armoured train mounting a 7 pounder muzzle-loading naval gun. On 15 November, with over 160 men aboard, it left Frere for Estcourt, where, seeing no enemy, its commander decided to go on another seven miles to

Chieveley. As it chugged noisily through the countryside, Botha's men spotted it and quickly blocked the line behind it. On its return journey most of the trucks were derailed but, after a heroic stand, the engine was freed and sped back with two wagons carrying 90 men, 70 of them wounded. Of the remainder, five were killed and the rest, including Winston Churchill, war correspondent for the *Morning Post*, were captured.

Unmolested, the Boer expedition, which looted with enthusiasm, moved on towards Frere, where it split. On 21 November, the two groups joined hands again between Frere and the Mooi River. By now General Hildyard at Estcourt and General Barton at Mooi River had each more troops than Joubert, who was nevertheless credited by the British with 7,000 men. In an excess of caution, partly engendered by lack of information and maps, the two generals failed to concert any action against the Boers, other than an ineffective night encounter at Willow Grange in which only a tiny proportion of their forces managed to engage the enemy. But Buller claimed it to be a brilliant victory.

Dispirited by the signs of British reinforcements, and by dreadful weather, Joubert ordered a withdrawal behind the Tugela and, laden with loot, this was slowly accomplished by 28 November, without British interference. Viljoen wrote angrily that, 'two Boers had been struck by lightning, which, according to his [Joubert's] doctrine, was an infallible sign from the Almighty that the commandos were to proceed no further', thus the expedition was recalled. For the rest of November and the first fortnight of December, the British assembled an ever-growing number of men and quantity of stores round Frere in preparation for their relief of Ladysmith.

CHAPTER FIVE

Black Week

'You should see our entrenchments . . . we come out of our burrows and simply shoot them down like deer. . . . It is not war, but it is magnificent.'
From a surprising letter written by an Englishman fighting with the Boers at Magersfontein.

'The Boers could never win the war because they could not follow up a success.'
V. Sampson and Ian Hamilton, Anti-Commando.

Between a Sunday and the following Friday, the Boers repulsed the British army on three battlefields. The first to suffer defeat was Gatacre at Stormberg in Cape Colony on 10 December; the following day Methuen endured the same fate at Magersfontein, and Buller completed the series at Colenso on 15 December. On none of these occasions did the Boers follow up their successes, but fought purely defensive battles from very strong positions which the British generals had not even cursorily reconnoitred before attacking. The total British casualties amounted to about 380 killed, 1,550 wounded and 860 taken prisoner, while the Boers lost perhaps 100 killed, 250 wounded and a few dozen prisoners. (It was symbolic of the time that these relatively minor setbacks to the might of the British Empire caused far more stir and shock both at home and abroad than did the slaughter at Passchendaele in 1917.) Stormberg can hardly be dignified with the title of a battle; rather was it an ill-managed skirmish. In its conception and its execution it was characteristic of Gatacre, whom Lyttelton said 'was as brave as a lion . . . No day was too hot for him, no hours too long, no work too hard. But he was very jealous of authority, he wanted to do everything himself and was very fond of the sound of his own voice.' Although enjoining caution, Buller gave Gatacre a free hand. By December, the British troops outnumbered the Boers, whose commander, Olivier, showed little inclination to employ his 3,000 men aggressively. Indeed he only entered Stormberg on 25 November, three weeks after Buller had ordered its evacuation, but its loss meant that Gatacre's lateral communication link with French was severed. On 9 December Gatacre had assembled 3,000 troops near Molteno and planned to recapture Stormberg. He decided on a night approach march of about 10 miles over rough country before launching a bayonet charge, under cover of darkness, up the steep rocky sides of the Kissieberg ridge which dominates the railway and is situated two and a half miles south-west of Stormberg. It was known that the Boers had a laager here, but he hoped to surprise them.

In the words of Roberts, Gatacre displayed 'a want of care, judgement and even of ordinary military precautions'. For instance, the route had not been reconnoitred, the officer who knew the district best did not accompany the column, no proper maps were available, and some of the troops, including Reservists who had only very recently arrived from England, had been employed all day in the heat on heavy fatigue duties. The start of the march was delayed for two hours, and then the leading guides soon lost their way in the dark. The rear of the column took the correct route, but having lost all contact with the main body, decided to return to Molteno which they had almost reached before being sent back. Nevertheless, the extremely tired troops did fortuitously reach the right place. Dawn was breaking when the Boers observed the soldiers who, with the indefatigable Gatacre leading them, were marching through a defile with bayonets fixed and in column of fours. Despite these handicaps, the Irish Rifles gained their objectives on Kissieberg ridge, but were shortly afterwards fired on by their own guns and their commanding officer was mortally wounded. The Fusiliers, confronted by a far more precipitous climb, were unable to get more than half-way up the ridge, and some of them scrambled back into the valley. Seeing this withdrawal, Gatacre ordered a return to Molteno. Although the Boers harassed the infantry, most of them were safely extricated with the help of the artillery and mounted troops. But, in the confusion, nobody noticed that over half the Fusiliers were unaccounted for; many had either fallen asleep, exhausted, or been unwilling to risk the descent, and nearly 600 were made prisoners; in addition, 25 men were killed and 110 wounded; Boer losses were negligible. Gatacre's incompetence was further illustrated by the map he produced five weeks later for his official account, which placed the battle beyond Stormberg, over four miles to the north of where the encounter happened.

On the front facing Methuen, the Boers had to settle some pressing problems, the most immediate being the quarrel between the Transvaalers and the Free Staters. Understandably Cronje complained strongly to Kruger about the feeble performance of the Free State troops which led to their hasty withdrawal at the Modder River battle. Kruger appealed to Steyn to rally his soldiers, concluding his message in Cromwellian language: 'Honour must impress upon officers and burghers that they must hold out to the death in the name of the Lord!' In consequence, Steyn went from Bloemfontein to the front where he spent several days impressing on his countrymen the need to stand firm, thereby healing this dispute.

The second matter concerned abortive guerrilla action behind Methuen's lines. On the night of 6 December, Prinsloo, with three guns, attacked Enslin station, but was held at bay for several hours by two companies of the Northamptonshire Regiment (about 200 men), until reinforcements arrived, when the Boers gave up. The damage to the railway track was slight, and for his incompetent leadership Prinsloo was sacked as Commandant-General, Ferreira being elected in his place. This change of command greatly improved the Free Staters' morale at the crucial moment, prior to the forthcoming battle.

The third and most important problem facing the Boer leaders was where best to make their final stand before Kimberley. With the reinforcements from Natal, Cronje had about 7,000 men (the British estimate was 15,000). He intended to occupy the Spytfontein heights, where some defences had already been constructed, but having surveyed them, de la Rey insisted on Magersfontein where the British would have to approach the Boer lines over open ground, and, supported by Steyn, his proposals carried the day at a *Kriegsraad* [council of war] only a week before the battle.

On 4 December the Boers began to occupy and construct defensive positions along a twelve-mile diagonal line whose axis was north-west to south-east. Because the Magersfontein defences were greatly strengthened and elaborated during the next twelve weeks, any description of their state prior to the battle must be tentative. The many barbed wire entanglements of later photographs did not then exist. On the battlefield were only two wire fences, one marking a farm boundary; the other, more substantial one, delineating the Orange Free State border, was outside most of the fighting zone, being four miles to the east of the railway.

The Boer line began at the Langeberg farm and this sector stretched eastwards to the railway; it was fairly lightly held by Andreas Cronje, Piet's brother, and in this sector little was to happen. In the centre of the position, and dominating the flat ground, is the steep 200 feet high Magersfontein kopje which has been likened to a large stranded whale, and measures about a mile in length, running in a north-south direction. Incorporating this natural strongpoint within their defensive system, the Boers dug 1,000 yards of four-feet-deep slit trenches about 150 yards forward of the kopje's southern face. These trenches were not in a continuous line. They were expertly sited and camouflaged, giving their occupiers an excellent field of fire and almost complete immunity from rifle and shell fire. On the kopje itself, stone sangars and other trenches had been openly prepared to hoodwink the British into believing that the main concentration of troops would, as at Belmont and Graspan, be on these heights. This central sector extended for over three miles, from the railway to the eastern face of the kopje; the troops there were commanded by Piet Cronje. Next came a gap, where a small force of Sandinavian volunteers was posted. The south-eastern flank was the longest and conformed to the line of a very low ridge, well covered with scrub, which reached almost to the river, but little had been done to improve the natural advantages of this inconspicuous feature. Finally, Boers held both sides of the Modder at Moss Drift and placed one of their guns on the southern bank, but most of their artillery and pom-poms were concentrated on or around the kopje. For the Boers, these defences were revolutionary, the trenches in the centre having no avenue of retreat if things went wrong. This was to be a fight to the finish and so confident of success was de la Rey, that, though commanding the south-eastern sector, he went, on 9 December, to Kimberley to comfort his wife over the death of their son.

Although tired after their exertions culminating in the Modder River battle of 28 November, the British sluggishness between then and 11 December was inexcusable. Before the Boers recovered their morale, no attempt was made to deny them Magersfontein (a cavalry patrol had ridden across it unscathed on 4 December), nor was any effort made to push on the few miles up the Modder to seize Moss Drift (not fortified till 8 December). Instead a little desultory patrolling was ordered, while reinforcements and supplies were arriving and the railway bridge was being repaired. Since he now knew that Kimberley could hold out for another forty days, it is difficult to find much justification for Methuen's timing of the forthcoming battle. What seems to have most influenced Methuen was the conviction that his all-Regular division, now 15,000 strong, could again compel the Boers to relinquish any defensive positions they might have constructed.

For his continued advance, Methuen had three possible routes, but two of these suffered from grave drawbacks. With his limited resources, the arid countryside west of the railway precluded him from sending a large body of men round this way to outflank the Boers. The prospects on the east were more superficially attractive, and, at first, Methuen proposed breaking out in this direction, but was dissuaded because his troops would have been very vulnerable to enfilading fire from the Magersfontein area and from across the river. Also the Orange Free State boundary fence formed an unpleasant obstacle along the whole of this front. Even if the troops succeeded in by-passing the Magersfontein positions, it was feared that the Modder bridge and the railway line would have been easy targets for counter-attacks by Boers who could infiltrate behind the main body of the British forces. Thus Methuen decided to advance frontally over the open veld. With no skilled scouts and with cavalry patrols unable to approach close enough to gain up-to-date knowledge of the enemy disposition, he had little reliable information of the whereabouts of the Boer positions. Yet, on 11 December, a captive balloon was due to go into service with his division, but Methuen did not consider postponing the attack until after it had arrived.

On 7 December Methuen issued his plans. On 10 December a softening-up bombardment by 23 guns, including a 4·7 in. naval gun and a battery of 6 in. howitzers, concentrated on the kopje for over an hour and a half, producing a magnificent spectacle of flying rocks and dust, all enveloped in the yellow lyddite smoke from the 4·7 in. gun's shells. The experts thought that nothing could have survived this pounding, but only three Boer soldiers had been wounded and, assured that this was the spot chosen for the impending attack, Cronje and all available troops took up their positions as night fell. The main British attack was entrusted to Wauchope's newly arrived Highland Brigade. Its four regiments were to make a night march of less than three miles as the crow flies, followed by a dawn attack on the southern and eastern sides of the Magersfontein kopje. By enveloping and capturing this height, the British would have split the Boer positions into two, rendering them untenable. The Guards Brigade was to protect the eastern, while most of 9th Brigade screened Wauchope's western flank. No alternative plans were drawn up should the Highland Brigade's attack fail.

As usual, Methuen gave his subordinate, Wauchope, freedom to choose his method of getting into position and fighting the engagement, once there. A fine soldier, Wauchope was apparently unhappy about the role allotted to his brigade, but made no official representations to Methuen, so one must assume that he reckoned the task to have been within the competence of his force. His most exacting problem was to keep nearly 4,000 men together in a night march over ground liberally strewn with many obstacles, such as large boulders, anthills and thick clumps of prickly bushes.

At 00.30 hours the brigade started from Headquarters Hill in a thunderstorm. Its deployment was in mass of quarter column which meant a compact rectangular body of troops formed up into 90 lines, each of about 40 men, measuring about 45 yards wide by 330 yards deep. The theoretical speed of this human phalanx was one mile per hour. This should have permitted a brief rest before beginning the difficult movement into extended order, which was intended to spread the force over a front of 2,500 yards and be completed before dawn. Relying on compass bearings, the march was guided by Major Benson, Royal Artillery, who had previously and courageously reconnoitred most of the route on foot. Accompanying him on the left of the column was Wauchope. Of the effects of the natural obstacles on the march, a survivor recalled, 'We were tacking about in the

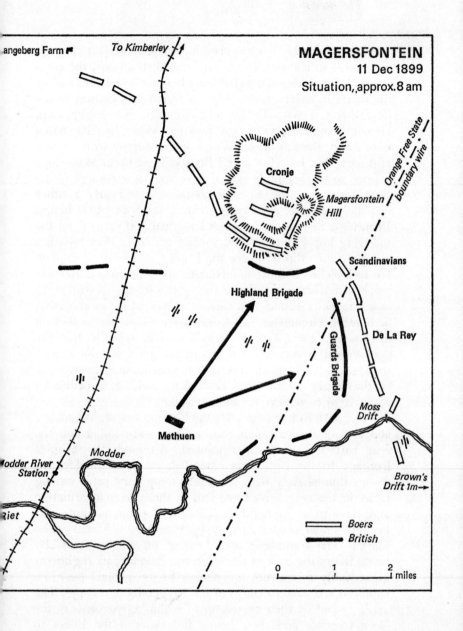

MAGERSFONTEIN

11 Dec 1899

Situation, approx. 8 am

angeberg Farm

To Kimberley

Cronje

Magersfontein Hill

Orange Free State boundary wire

Scandinavians

Highland Brigade

De La Rey

Guards Brigade

Moss Drift

Methuen

Modder

Modder River Station

Riet

Brown's Drift 1m→

Boers

British

0   1   2

miles

most extraordinary way and making frequent stops to change direction'. In addition to the physical obstructions, the compasses were rendered unreliable by ironstone boulders and by the metal in nearly 4,000 rifles. Nevertheless Benson somehow directed the Highlanders, through the heavy rain, almost on to their prearranged position. When less than half a mile away, Benson urged Wauchope to deploy while it was still dark, but he refused and Benson went back. Wauchope wanted to be absolutely sure that he was close enough to the Boer lines, and the advance continued for nearly another quarter of a mile. As daylight came, at about 04.00 hours, Wauchope had reached a point less than 500 yards from the towering kopje and just 300 yards from some Boer trenches and only then did he order the leading regiment to deploy. He had picked a most unfortunate spot, because a sizeable patch of bushes compelled many of the troops to scatter, in order to skirt round this thicket. Thus what, in the most favourable circumstances, would have been a complicated manœuvre, got off to a very bad start. Hardly had the deployment begun when rifle fire poured from the hidden trenches. Initially much of it went too high, but it threw some of the weary troops into confusion, making co-ordinated action hard to achieve for the next hour.

A quarter of an hour after the fighting began, Wauchope and two of the battalion commanders were killed and the rear battalion commander injured. Although the brigade frontage to the right was extended, some of the forward troops immediately fled, spreading temporary panic among many in the rear, who were still in their massed formation and thus most vulnerable. This near pandemonium was brought under control, partly by Pipe-Major Mackay who played 'The Campbells are Coming' on his bagpipes. By 06.00 hours the bulk of the Highland Brigade, its regiments inextricably mixed up, lay pinned to the ground near the southern and eastern edges of the Magersfontein kopje. The artillery had by then moved up to within 2,000 yards of the Boer trenches and their heavy fire reduced the Boers to silence. In the intense heat, there now existed a stalemate very similar to that of the Modder River battle.

The rest of this battle was dominated by the predicament into which the Highland Brigade had been plunged. Once he had appreciated their plight, Methuen temporarily filled the dangerous gap on the Highlanders' eastern flank with an artillery battery, and some dismounted horsemen who kept the Boers from making any forward movement from the low ridge until the Guards Brigade had been deployed. Not daring to risk this Brigade, Methuen gave Colvile no orders to make an immediate attack which, since the Boers held the ridge with very few troops, might have led to their collapse here, and possibly saved the Highland Brigade from disaster. At the southern end of the line by the Modder, a small mixed force of cavalry and infantry could only make a limited impression against determined Boer resistance. On the western flank, two battalions from 9th Brigade advanced to about level with the Magersfontein kopje but, as Pole-Carew had only been ordered to throw a screen forward to protect the Modder River camp, he did not seek out the enemy who were weak here. The artillery continued to play a decisive part in the battle, with the observers in the balloons (which arrived that morning), finding some good targets, including over 200 Boer ponies.

By 10.00 hours the battle had become almost static, with Methuen having committed nearly all his troops. He still anticipated that the Highland Brigade would not have to withdraw till nightfall and that, as at the Modder River, the Boers would then have pulled out. The observers in the balloon reported, however, that the Boers were being steadily reinforced. On the British side, a trickle of Highlanders ran the gauntlet of snipers' bullets, both to escape from the enemy and from the scorching sun. Methuen now strengthened the Highland Brigade by employing his only reserve. At about 11.00 hours, half a battalion dashed forward to join their fellow Scots, only to be halted by the Boers. Nothing had been gained and another lull ensued.

The retreat of the Highlanders was precipitated by a counter-attack at 13.30 hours against the eastern extremity of their position. Seeing this enfilading movement, Hughes-Hallett, the most senior officer surviving, ordered two companies to pivot back. This apparent withdrawal became a signal for a general retreat, temporarily degenerating into a stampede, into which the Boers poured rifle fire. 'Then I saw a sight that I hope I may never see again; men of the Highland Brigade running for all they were worth, others cowering under bushes . . . officers running about with revolvers in their hands threatening to shoot them, urging on some, kicking on others; staff officers galloping about giving incoherent and impracticable orders,' wrote an officer. As these overwrought men crowded round carts carrying food and water, the Boer artillery shelled this perfect target, and the Highland Brigade disintegrated. Finally, the Guards and most of the Artillery spent the night near where they had been fighting, but Pole-Carew's battalions were withdrawn. The Boers, exhausted and short of ammunition, stayed in their positions; Magersfontein was not a repetition of the Modder River.

On 12 December an armistice was soon arranged, but this news did not reach those manning the 4·7 in. gun who fired at the Boers as they climbed out of their trenches. In retaliation, the Boers shelled G Battery who waited calmly without replying until the ceasefire message was understood by both sides. The Boers blindfolded the British medical teams, but were most considerate in helping to collect the dead and wounded. That afternoon, with the armistice over, the Guards, in impeccable order, marched back in slow time to the Modder River and although the Boer artillery opened fire, they carefully avoided hitting these easy targets, for they were white men, not bent on harming other white men.

Methuen lost 7% of his division and expended most of its ammunition. Out of about 950 casualties (210 killed), 750 were in the Highland Brigade, the Black Watch losing 60%

of its officers and 37% of its other ranks. The Boers lost about 90 killed, mainly the Scandinavians, and 188 wounded. Buller's reaction was typical; he told Methuen he could retreat to the Orange River Station from whence the division had set out three weeks before. At a council of war, however, Pole-Carew persuaded Methuen against this abject step and the division settled down to recuperate by the contaminated waters of the Modder.

The humiliation of Stormberg and the defeat of the illustrious Highland Brigade at Magersfontein shook the British nation. But sombre though the scene was, it was universally believed that Buller would soon retrieve the situation. Bennet Burleigh, of the *Daily Telegraph,* summed up this feeling: 'He will quickly put an end to the existing deplorable situation. He is a stern, fighting soldier, as well as an experienced and masterly leader of troops, who will stand no nonsense nor brook incapables. With him in the field the Boers' long innings [*sic*] will be finally closed.'

Although Buller had arrived in Natal on 25 November, his presence was at first kept secret. His position there was an anomalous one because Clery still nominally retained the command of 2nd Division. By early December four infantry brigades, 44 guns, including 14 of the longer range naval weapons, and about 1,800 cavalry, mainly locally raised formations, totalling 18,000 combatant troops, had been assembled at Frere, a mere 25 miles south, as the crow flies, from Ladysmith. But blocking the way was the formidable natural barrier of the Tugela Heights and holding its strongholds were at least 5,000 well-armed troops (Buller's estimate was 20,000), led by the able 37-year-old Louis Botha.

As he had no accurate maps, nor was close reconnaissance easy, Buller's chief problem was where to breach the Boer lines. The most direct and obvious route was near or at Colenso, but once the British were across the deep swift-flowing Tugela River, they would find themselves entrapped within a semi-circular range of wild, almost trackless hills, six miles across and about five miles deep, rising 500–1,000 feet above the river. Any approach march would be easily visible to the defenders who can be compared to soldiers manning high cliffs, waiting to repel invaders who have first to cross a large exposed beach. Buller, therefore, soon decided to outflank Colenso by crossing at Potgieter's Drift, about 25 miles upstream. But this meant leaving the railway and, being short of transport, there would be delays while stores were being transferred. Furthermore it was impossible to hide such a move, and the Boers, with inside lines, could easily switch their forces to new and strong positions opposite this proposed crossing place. Nevertheless a feint attack towards Colenso could be expected to pin down a sizeable proportion of the enemy, and the British out-numbered the Boers both in men and artillery.

Buller learnt of Methuen's defeat on 13 December and cancelled this plan. Apparently feeling that a quick victory was essential, he switched the offensive to Colenso. During 13–14 December the British forces moved forward beyond Chieveley where, as before Magersfontein, the artillery shelled dummy Boer gun positions, Botha having moved them the previous night, after an artillery officer had deserted to the British. Always convinced that Buller would attack here, Botha had carefully prepared a trap. The key to the Boer defensive positions was the 550-feet-high Hlangwani Mountain feature. Its exact location relative to the Tugela is most deceptive, because up to Colenso the river flows in an easterly direction, but then, just as it reaches Hlangwani, it turns sharply northwards for several miles. To the British observers on the southern side, the course of the Tugela was invisible, the river bed being 25 feet or more below the banks.

Nine years later, Botha took de la Rey, Smuts, Schalk Burger and Sir Percy FitzPatrick on a battlefield tour of Colenso. Botha recalled that he had been forced to persuade his men to reoccupy the posts they had earlier quitted on Hlangwani. 'Well, how was I going to get our people to occupy a hill close on Buller's flank, with a flooded river

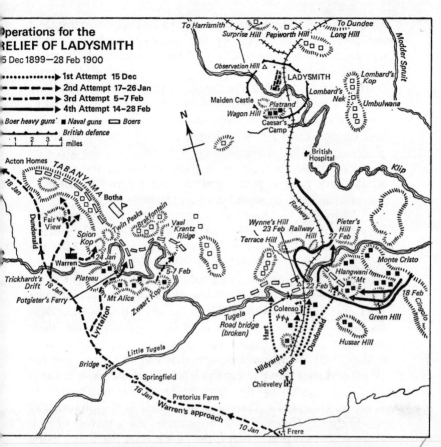

Operations for the RELIEF OF LADYSMITH
5 Dec 1899—28 Feb 1900

••••••••••► 1st Attempt 15 Dec
– – – – ► 2nd Attempt 17–26 Jan
–•–•–•► 3rd Attempt 5–7 Feb
━━━━► 4th Attempt 14–28 Feb

Boer heavy guns ■ Naval guns ◻ Boers

⌣⌣⌣⌣ British defence

1 2 3 4 miles

behind them and no line of retreat? . . . Each one would ask why he must be sent there. No, they would simply refuse or saddle up and go home.' Botha convened a war council of the leaders of the 13 Commandos, all of whom were older than he. After a long discussion, they agreed on the vital importance of Hlangwani and the choice fell on Red Joshua Joubert to go there, who exclaimed, 'The choice of the lot is the choice of God! I go', and he and his men swam the flooded river to occupy Hlangwani. Botha's plan was that 'no one was to fire until the signal was given by me. Our heavy guns were to remain concealed and to reserve their fire, and our burghers posted all along the hills were on no account to fire and expose their positions. This was particularly so in the case of those on Hlangwani. You see we had destroyed the railway bridge, but not the road bridge, and the plan was to draw the enemy on to that open flat across the river and to wait until all or most of them had crossed by the road bridge and then to open fire with canon and rifle on top of them. With the flooded river, then behind them, and the force on Hlangwani to attack them in flank and rear, the position would have been hopeless and the whole force would have been annihilated, or would have had to surrender.'

Despite some cursory reconnaissance, Buller had little knowledge of the area. His vague and brief orders for a head-on attack on Colenso reflected the hasty way in which the operation was arranged. Under Clery's fictitious authority the actual battle orders were only issued on the night of 14 December, so that those leading the troops could not even scan the ground over which they were to advance next morning. Some extracts from Buller's orders show their ambiguity. Hart's brigade (4th) was to cross the Tugela at Bridle Drift (there were several drifts in this section of the river) and then move along the left bank of the river towards the kopje north of the iron bridge. The other leading brigade, Hildyard's (2nd) was to 'march in the direction of the bridge at Colenso' and cross there. As a matter of fact, there were two iron bridges, the blown road one being half a mile upstream from the rail bridge. Barton's brigade (6th) was to 'move at 4 a.m. east of the railway where it can protect the right flank of the 2nd Brigade and if necessary support the mounted troops'. These were Dundonald's force of 1,000 men who were to try 'to take up a position on Hlangwani Hill'. The main artillery, twelve field guns and six naval 12 pounders under Colonel Long and Lieutenant Ogilvy, RN, were to move off at 03.30 hours 'under cover of 6th Brigade to a point which it can prepare the crossing for the 2nd Brigade'. Notice that both infantry brigades were

only to begin their advance at 4 a.m. Having left them in
Cape Town, Buller himself had no proper staffs, and he never
informed White of his new plan, so that the Ladysmith
garrison, not expecting any offensive till 17 December, had
no time to make a supporting sortie.

Commander Limpus, commanding the two 4·7 in. and
four 12 pounder naval guns, described how, on the previous
night, Captain Jones, RN, who was in charge of the Naval
Brigade, 'electrified us by announcing that at 2.30 a.m.
Friday 15 December we were to strike camp again and move
forward with the whole force at 4 a.m. to a position 3,500
yds from the enemy, shell him while the infantry Brigades
advanced and then cross the river behind them! . . . to move
at all we had to catch and inspan 22 teams, each of 18 oxen,
strike camp, pack our belongings (240 of us) on to wagons
. . . We breakfasted at 2.45 and at 4 a.m. sharp moved off.
Needless to say we went absolutely alone, the others being "a
little late". The staff officers, however, spotted us and
pranced after us and halted us to await the remainder in the
open plain, in full view of, and within easy range of, the
enemy's guns. I was really quite alarmed for our battery, but
the only thing to do was to sit down and laugh.' He continues, 'At 5 a.m. we were at our place, got the teams out-
spanned, and at 5.20 opened fire. No reply for about 20
minutes. On went the Infantry, etc, until about 5.40 the
battle began in earnest.'

What Limpus heard was Botha's men disobeying their
orders by opening fire spontaneously on some of the most
enticing targets imaginable. The brave but stupid Hart
marched his men in massed quarter column, in daylight
towards the enemy. His native guide disappeared, leaving
Hart to forge on into a loop of the Tugela not shown on his
map. Here his Irish brigade was caught by intensive cross-
fire, at first somewhat wild and inaccurate, which permitted
the troops to disperse, against Hart's instructions, and take
advantage of what cover existed. A handful of men managed
to cross the fast-flowing river, but by 07.00 hours the rest,

as at the Modder River and Magersfontein, were pinned down. Buller reacted to this by saying, 'Hart has got into a devil of a mess down there,' and telling Lyttelton to use the reserve brigade to extricate Hart.

In the centre, both Hildyard's and Barton's brigades were very slow off the mark and, like Limpus, Long soon found himself in front of the infantry. Determined to give adequate support with his relatively short-range guns, Long had, by 06.00 hours, advanced to within 1,000 yards of the Tugela and began to bring the guns into action. Botha takes up the story again: 'I don't know if any of our men were premature and revealed their presence by shooting, but whatever it was, it was Colonel Long who saw them and realized that our force on Hlangwani was already across the river and there was grave danger of a flank attack, and he made it so hot that they had to open fire all along and so gave the whole plan away . . . They blamed him for the failure, blamed him for risking and losing his guns, but that man saved the British Army that day.'

Although the Boer fire was fierce and Long himself badly wounded, the gunners' casualties were not unduly heavy and they almost succeeded in silencing the Boer artillery; but at about 07.00 hours, running short of ammunition, they withdrew to a less exposed position nearby, to await the arrival of more ammunition. Their sudden silence seems to have struck Buller as a most ominous sign and he ordered the dilatory Hildyard to send support to the gun position, but not to let the infantry get involved in any fighting. The Devons and the Queens managed this task with little difficulty. In the meantime, Dundonald's small force was unable to make much impression on Hlangwani, but he requested Barton to send troops to the west of this feature to threaten the Boer avenue of retreat across the Tugela hoping that this move might dislodge them. Always un-enter-prising, Barton refused to co-operate.

By 09.00 hours the battle had become a stalemate. Although less than half his force was committed, Buller insisted on calling off the whole attack, which, after dark, could have been accomplished with little loss. Already despondent at Hart's failure, Buller became thoroughly alarmed when he met two officers, sent to obtain more ammunition, who assured him that Long's men and guns were knocked out. Deciding to see for himself, Buller fool-hardily rode forward from his headquarters, near Limpus' gun position. A shell burst almost on top of him, killing his doctor and bruising him painfully, but he continued un-deterred to observe the apparently abandoned guns, and from this sight he drew the most extreme conclusions. Suffering from shell shock, which made him distraught at the thought of more casualties, Buller's judgement deserted him and he speedily reduced the battle to a bloody fiasco. (For his reputation, and even more for the conduct of the campaign, it was tragic that he was neither killed nor completely incapacitated, as General Patton later cynically remarked, 'nobody blames a badly injured general'.) Ordering back ammunition wagons that were now approaching the guns, Buller demanded an immediate precipitate withdrawal and, to retrieve Long's guns, he called for volunteers. The response was immediate.

When recalling this scene, Botha became almost incoherent: 'I was on the hill above the bridge there and with the field glasses could see it all. All our people were watch-ing: it was a terrible thing to see, like looking down at a play from the gallery. When the teams and the men were shot down, just swept away by our fire . . . and when we saw another lot of men and more teams dash to work to save the guns we held our breath; it was madness; nothing could live there. Then came another lot, and another and another . . . I was sick with horror that such bravery should be so useless. God, I turned away and could not look; and yet I had to look again. It was too wonderful.'

Although Ogilvy managed to get the naval 12 pounders back, only two of the twelve field guns were saved, before Buller ordered these suicidal efforts to cease. (Among those killed was Roberts' only son who was awarded the Victoria Cross; his body was later brought back by the Natal Indian ambulance team with whom Mahatma Gandhi was serving.) By 11.00 hours nearly all the British forces were retreating almost unmolested and at 14.30 the large naval guns withdrew. The British lost 143 killed, 756 wounded, and 240 captured, nearly half being in Hart's brigade. Despite the fact that the naval guns alone fired over 1,000 shells, the Boer casualties were only six dead and 21 wounded. In despair, Buller heliographed to White, suggesting his 'firing away as much ammunition as you can, and making the best terms you can', a proposal that White spurned. Buller felt no compunction in laying most of the blame for his failure on his subordinates, especially the badly injured Long. Yet his prestige was so overwhelming that none of the senior officers, and Clery accompanied him throughout most of the battle, ventured to criticize his more outrageously foolish orders. Writing long afterwards, Lyttelton said, 'One would have thought that confidence in Buller would have been seriously impaired, but I cannot say that this was the case, certainly not among the men'.

CHAPTER SIX

Ladysmith Unrelieved;
Spion Kop and Vaal Krantz

'The only thing I ever really fear is a "wobble" in British opinion.'

Milner to Chamberlain, 17 January, 1900.

'The vast majority of German military experts believe that the South African war will end with a complete defeat of the English . . . Nobody here believes that the English will reach Pretoria.'

*Count von Bülow (German Foreign Minister,)
December, 1899.*

The battle of Colenso marked a turning point in the war. Like the whole nation, the Government responded to this new rebuff with a spirit of jingoistic determination. On the evening of 15 December Buller sent Landsdowne a pessimistic letter, and the Cabinet immediately replied, reminding him sternly that 'Her Majesty's Government regard the abandonment of White's force and its consequent surrender as a national disaster of the greatest magnitude'. On being told that he would be reinforced, Buller's nerve revived and he promised to renew his efforts to relieve Ladysmith. But the situation in South Africa clearly required more drastic measures and these the Government took with unusual promptitude and firmness. The dispatch of two more divisions, the 6th and 7th, was speeded up and it was announced that large numbers of volunteers, including

67

mounted men, would be enrolled both in Britain and the Colonies. These forces would be the largest Britain had ever sent overseas. Equally important, the command structure was reformed. Field-Marshal Lord Roberts was asked to leave Ireland to become Commander-in-Chief, South Africa. He nominated Kitchener as his Chief-of-Staff, who was still in the Sudan where he had won a great reputation. Knowing that both Queen Victoria and Wolseley, the Commander-in-Chief, disliked Roberts, the Cabinet never consulted them over his appointment. Although virtually superseded, Buller was not made to resign but remained as the autonomous commander in Natal. On 23 December Roberts sailed quietly from Southampton, arriving in Cape Town on 10 January, 1900.

For a month after Colenso, no major action was fought. In the west, Methuen sat by the Modder, while Cronje with 8,000 troops, many now joined by their families, leisurely strengthened the Magersfontein defences. In Kimberley, Kekwich, increasingly at odds with the frustrated Rhodes, was invested by Wessels' and Ferreira's 3,000 troops. Further north Snyman with 2,500 men continued to besiege Baden-Powell in Mafeking. On the Rhodesian border, Commandant Botha's force of about 1,000 men merely prevented Plumer from reaching Mafeking. Along the Orange Free State–Cape border, French's cavalry near Colesberg pursued a more vigorous, but necessarily cautious, policy against Schoeman's 5,000 troops. Further to the east, Gatacre, at Molteno, faced Grobelaar's 4,000 commandos who were based on Stormberg. But it was in Natal that both sides concentrated the major part of their forces. By mid-January, Buller's amounted to 32,000 men and Joubert's to more than 21,000, about 7,000 being detached under Botha to defend the Tugela Heights, the remainder besieging Ladysmith. Altogether the Boers had about 46,500 men in the field, of whom 6,000 were rebels, mostly recently recruited from Cape Colony. These were Afrikaans who were technically British citizens. By January, 1900, the

British had already sent out 120,000 men and reinforcements were pouring in. Thus the Boers' chances of winning the war had almost vanished.

Granted a free hand in Natal by Roberts, Buller now reverted to his plan of working round the western flank of the Boer positions to reach Ladysmith; and the recent assault there had increased the urgency for its relief. Buller's army had been greatly strengthened by the arrival of the 5th Division. It was commanded by Sir Charles Warren, a clever 58-year-old Engineer Officer notorious for his bad temper and eccentricity. Twenty years earlier he had had experience of South African native warfare and, latterly, after two stormy years as High Commissioner for the London Metropolitan Police, had been in Singapore as its first Commander-in-Chief where he and the Governor had squabbled bitterly. Despite these shortcomings, Wolseley had taken Warren out of retirement. To make matters worse, Wolseley had ostentatiously given Warren a 'Dormant Commission' to replace Buller should the latter be incapacitated. The two men mistrusted each other from the first, and Buller soon came to detest Warren, but had to employ him.

On 10 January, the Natal Army, about 24,000 strong with 58 guns, left their camps at Frere to embark on one of the most futile operations in the annals of warfare. Buller planned to cross the Tugela at Potgieter's Drift, some 15 miles upstream from Colenso, break through the hills there and relieve Ladysmith from the west. Accompanying the troops, on a shuttle service, were 325 wagons carrying the vast quantities of stores which Warren considered essential. Their line of march stretched for seventeen miles, its pace being reduced to one mile per hour as the thousands of horses, mules and oxen struggled to pull their loads through the rain-sodden ground which soon turned into a quagmire. From the heights on the other bank, the Boers surveyed this crawling mass and its cavalry spearhead. They soon realized Buller's plan and began to assemble on and to fortify the wide arc of hills dominating Potgieter's Drift. On 12 January

Buller climbed Mount Alice, 1,000 feet above the flooded Tugela. He could see the Boer defences being constructed on the opposite bank and discarded the idea of a full-scale attack here. Instead he decided to split his forces. At Potgieter's Drift, where Dundonald's cavalry had already seized the ferry, he placed Lyttelton with 9,000 men and the long-range naval guns. He ordered Lyttelton to cross the Tugela, but only to demonstrate against the Boers. The main thrust was to be made by Warren, whom Buller sent, with 15,000 troops, a further five miles upstream to Trickhardt's Drift. Thereby, he intended to turn the lightly held Boer western flank. On 15 January, Buller issued secret orders to Warren. They were vaguely worded, stating, 'You will of course act as circumstances require, but my idea is that you should continue throughout refusing your right, and throwing your left forward till you gain the open plain north of Spion Kop. Once there, you will command the rear of the position facing Potgieter's Drift, and I think render it untenable.' No mention was made of Lyttelton's role, nor of the need for a rapid advance.

Meanwhile the ponderous British build-up continued and this was completed on 16 January. That night Lyttelton made a crossing at Potgieter's Drift and captured some kopjes, which convinced the Boers that this was the area of the major British attack. Early the following morning, Warren reached the Tugela, crossing it unopposed at Trickhardt's Drift. A most methodical man whose motto might have been 'hurry slowly', Warren had very definite theories on warfare. One of these was to defer any fighting until every item of stores had been assembled nearby. He also intended that, before his unblooded troops started their real offensive, they should undertake a kind of three days' dress rehearsal to become acquainted with their adversaries. Holding very different ideas, and commanding his cavalry brigade, was the Earl of Dundonald. He had previously received separate orders from Buller to move rapidly round the unprotected Boer western flank. He was doing this when, on 18 January, the following message came from Warren, 'The G.O.C. as far as he can see finds that there are no cavalry whatever round the camp and nothing to prevent the oxen being swept away. (There were now 15,000 of these beasts dispersed and competing for the limited grazing.) You are to send 500 mounted men at once to be placed round the camp.' With his remaining 1,000 troopers, Dundonald resolutely pushed on. He ambushed a Boer patrol and, before the Boers could forestall him, had established himself near Acton Homes, in a commanding position on a track running towards Ladysmith. His plea for guns and reinforcements to exploit his success were ignored. Instead, on 19 January, Warren recalled Dundonald. He remonstrated that he was only obeying Buller's orders, but Warren, shouting directions at the drivers of wagons crossing the bridges, angrily repeated, 'I want you close to me'. The cavalry were thus withdrawn and misemployed. Dundonald nevertheless drove the Boers off the dominating Bastion Hill at the westerly edge of Tabanyama (Rangeworthy Heights). It was against Tabanyama, daily strengthened by Botha with troops from Ladysmith, that Warren directed his dress-rehearsal style of attacks on 20 and 21 January.

Meanwhile, refusing to take charge himself and acting as a kind of umpire, Buller grew restive at Warren's dilatoriness. Visiting him on 22 January, Buller presented an ultimatum. Warren must either attack on the western flank or retire across the Tugela; or, as an afterthought, Buller suggested he should take Spion Kop, the highest point in the region, towering over Warren's eastern flank. Equally casually, Warren agreed to take this peak, 1,470 feet high. No guides could be found, but early on 23 January, Warren tried to spy out a route up the precipitous slopes. Later that morning Buller, furious at another day's inaction, personally told Warren that either he must capture the peak that night or go back across the Tugela, and so Warren made hurried preparations for an immediate attack, the ultimate purpose of which was not clear to anyone in authority.

4

Major-General Woodgate was placed in charge of the 1,700 troops detailed to capture Spion Kop. On the night of 23/24 January this force was led up the almost trackless southern side of the peak by Colonel Thorneycroft. Driving off a Boer piquet who gave the alarm, Thorneycroft reached the summit, after a seven-hour climb, at 04.00 hours. Then from the mist-shrouded summit those below heard three cheers, the signal announcing the safe arrival of the leading troops. Only a very cursory reconnaissance was made before the soldiers tried to dig themselves in. But their tools were almost useless against the solid rock and no sandbags had been brought up. When the mist lifted at about 08.00 hours, the British found that the shallow trench they had so laboriously scraped out was in the centre of an exposed semi-circular plateau of about 40 acres. Shaped like a boomerang and 300 yards long, this isolated main trench faced north and east. Into it were packed most of the soldiers, who were easily visible from nearby positions. Botha immediately appreciated this grave threat to the whole of his defences and, during the brief period of early morning mist, he dispatched riflemen to seize vantage points. It became a lovely clear day; and well-placed Boer marksmen began to enfilade the right flank of the trench from only 300 yards distance. Six guns and two pom-poms were brought up to pound the huddled British troops, causing very heavy casualties. By 10.00 hours, small parties of Boers had worked their way up to the lip of the plateau. From the dead ground there they began attacking the more outlying British detachments. Woodgate was mortally wounded, but co-ordinated control was in any case almost impossible. During the latter part of the morning, British reinforcements were filtered in. They helped their exhausted comrades, who continued to repulse the Boer attacks. But at about 13.00 hours the strain proved too much and some soldiers surrendered. A more complete collapse was only prevented by the personal intervention of Thorneycroft who rallied the faint-hearted, and the bitter struggle was resumed.

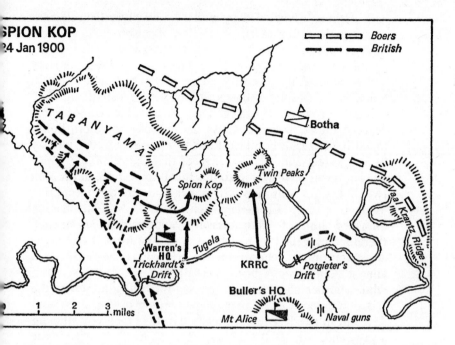

Buller had a panoramic view of the battle which was raging five miles north of his observation post on Mount Alice. Warren, on the other hand, was in a valley two miles west of Spion Kop and could observe nothing. No cable was laid, the heliograph was soon smashed, and thus Warren had to rely on messengers to bring him belated news of what was happening on Spion Kop. Nevertheless even when he had become aware of the critical situation, Warren never ordered a diversionary attack on Tabanyama which could have helped relieve the pressure on Spion Kop. Hence he kept 10,000 troops idle all that day, even though they were facing an enemy who had depleted his forces. Moreover, Warren believed that his troops occupied the whole summit, and thus he requested that Limpus' two big naval guns on Mount Alice should stop firing, so this one valuable artillery support ceased.

Although forbidden by Buller to do more than demonstrate at Potgieter's Drift, Lyttelton offered to help Warren. Warren agreed, and two fresh battalions were sent into the battle. One went to Spion Kop. The other crossed the river and scrambled up the very steep slopes two miles east of Spion Kop. Despite Buller's attempts to recall them, they valiantly drove the Boers off Twin Peaks which considerably reduced the enfilading fire. As the morning wore on, Buller found it increasingly difficult not to interfere. About midday he suggested, and Warren agreed, that the relatively junior Thorneycroft be placed in command at Spion Kop, but it took two hours for this news to reach him. In the meantime, Warren sent up Lieutenant-General Coke without having informed him of Thorneycroft's appointment. Confusion therefore prevailed as to who was in command. During the afternoon more reinforcements arrived. This resulted in almost 2,500 troops being packed into the actual summit, while another 2,000 waited just below. Still ignorant of the crisis on Spion Kop, Warren began issuing plans for the next day. But in the darkness, a steady trickle of men was slipping away and, at 20.00 hours, Thorneycroft ordered the abandonment of the hill. Coming down, Thorneycroft met Winston Churchill, who had already visited Spion Kop. Churchill was now returning with directions from Warren for Thorneycroft to hang on, but he replied, 'I have done all I can, and I am not going back'.

On the other side, the situation was strangely similar. Reitz describes the fighting: 'The English troops lay so near that one could have tossed a biscuit among them, and whilst the losses which they were causing us were only too evident, we on our side did not know that we were inflicting even greater damage upon them. Our own casualties lay hideously among us, but theirs were screened from view behind the breast-work.' As the day wore on, the Boers became disheartened and many deserted. At nightfall they retreated, not knowing that the British were doing the same. Reitz continues: 'We fully believed that the morning would see

them streaming through the breach to the relief of Ladysmith.' Only Botha had grasped the reality of the situation.
He implored the weary men to return immediately, which
many did. Next morning the Boers were horrified, because,
in Reitz's words, 'there cannot have been many battlefields
where there was such an accumulation of horrors within so
small a compass'. Both sides agreed to an armistice to bury
the dead and collect the wounded. The British had lost nearly
1,300, of whom over 350 were killed, and the Boers about
300. On the same day Buller took over from Warren, whom
he blamed for this disaster. He ordered a withdrawal across
the Tugela which was accomplished by 27 January without
any Boer interference.

Although Roberts had now asked him to remain on the
defensive, Buller made a third attempt to relieve Ladysmith,
whose garrison was being increasingly weakened by disease
and privation. By capturing Vaal Krantz Ridge, about four
miles east of Spion Kop, Buller hoped to unlock the Tugela
position. On 5 February, after massive artillery preparations
and an elaborate feint attack had alerted the Boers, he
unwillingly permitted Lyttelton to seize Vaal Krantz itself.
Then he suspended operations till next day. When Boer
resistance began to stiffen, he was assailed by doubts. He
telegraphed Roberts for advice, who told him to persevere,
but Buller's over-caution prevailed and he did nothing. On
7 February, after a meeting with his generals, most of whom
felt that the momentum was irretrievably lost, he abandoned
the operation. On 8 February the troops safely recrossed the
Tugela for the second time. Chiefly because he took such a
personal interest in their welfare, Buller's reputation and
popularity among his own troops survived this fiasco. With
no obvious replacement for Buller, Roberts may have
flinched from dismissing the General whose incompetence
had caused the death of his only son. Anyhow Buller remained
in command in Natal.

CHAPTER SEVEN

The Relief of Kimberley and Battle of Paardeberg

'Seven—six—eleven—five—nine-an'-twenty mile to-day—
Four—eleven—seventeen—thirty-two the day before—
(Boots—boots—boots—boots, movin' up and down again!)'
Kipling, Boots. (*The Connaught Rangers estimated that
they had marched 4774 miles during the Boer War*)

'Three days "to learn equitation",

. . .

I used to be in the Yorkshires once
(Sussex, Lincolns, and Rifles once),
Hampshires, Glosters, and Scottish once!
But now I am M.I.'
Kipling, M.I. (*Mounted Infantry of the Line*).

In contrast with Buller's floundering efforts in Natal, Roberts was already putting the finishing touches to a meticulously prepared offensive. He resolved to avoid another head-on attack against the Boers' strongly fortified positions. Instead, he planned an outflanking march against the Free State capital, Bloemfontein, starting on 12 February. But at the last minute, Roberts had to switch his thrust in order to relieve Kimberley where a serious rift between Kekwich and Rhodes led to unfounded fears that Rhodes wanted to surrender.

Until just beforehand Roberts only divulged his intentions to ten senior officers and railway officials, all directly involved in the planning. His main problem was administrative. Along the railway at Graspan and 18 miles further north at Modder River Station, he had concentrated, by early February, nearly 37,000 soldiers and 14,000 horses. This force had to be able to fight and provide itself with ammunition and food for at least a fortnight, up to 60 miles from the railhead, in the height of summer, and across large stretches of almost waterless country.

Throughout this campaign, the limiting factor for conventional forces operating at any distance from the railway was the carrying capacity and pace of supply wagons. For this relief operation, Kitchener was ordered to centralize the transport by removing the mule carts from regimental control and placing them under the Army Service Corps. The 21 infantry brigades, or their equivalents, were now each supported by a company of 125 native drivers with 50 carts, each being drawn by 10 mules. Every cart carried two days' supply of food. The mules could cover 16–18 miles daily, but had to carry their own forage. Locally obtainable, the oxen could pull far greater loads, and subsisted entirely by grazing, but they only did this during daylight, which meant that their maximum daily distance of 12 miles had to be partially covered at night. Needing over 1,300 native drivers, the six ox companies each had 100 wagons. These were drawn by a span of 16 oxen and transported more than three days' rations per man for the whole army. Much of the success of Roberts' plan hinged on this vulnerable transport system, comprising nearly 4,000 native drivers, about 11,000 mules, 9,600 oxen and over 1,700 wagons, all of which could be given little protection.

Roberts' cover plan was excellently conceived and executed. French's cavalry division had so effectively threatened Norval Pont bridge over the Orange River that the Boers continued to reinforce this area. They expected Roberts to choose the direct route to Bloemfontein, this being widely known as the plan officially favoured by the British. Even when French's division went to the Modder River, joining Kelly-Kenny's 6th Division, this move was construed as reinforcing Methuen for another attack on the Magersfontein positions. Early in February, a sizeable British force was sent to Koodesberg Drift, on the Modder, where it engaged the Boers for three days. This division helped persuade the Boers that any flank march for the relief of Kimberley would be to the west and not to the east of Magersfontein. Finally, Cronje was convinced that no British army would risk moving more than a few miles from its rail lifeline, and thus he discounted threats of a wide outflanking march on his eastern flank.

For this outflanking march to Kimberley the main jumping off point was Ramdam, with its plentiful water supply. Here, about 10 miles east of the railway at Graspan, most of his army converged, according to a strict timetable. In the lead was French's cavalry division, reinforced to 8,000 men who made a 20-mile preliminary march from their camps by the Modder River. They were to advance by three bounds; first, they were to seize drifts over the Riet River, 15 miles east of Ramdam, waiting there for the arrival of the leading infantry division. In their second and longest bound, they were to swing northward over 25 miles of waterless terrain to capture fords across the Modder River, about 15 miles to the east of Magersfontein, and again pause till the infantry caught up with them. In the final bound of 20 miles, they were to continue northwards to relieve Kimberley itself. The cavalry, with over 40 guns, was to leave Ramdam on 11 February, with six days' rations for the men and five days' forage for the horses. If this bold plan was to succeed, French's cavalry had to cover more than 80 miles at the hottest period of the year in less than five days. Speed was essential for confusing the Boer intelligence, but this flanking march, shaped like a huge letter J, would at first give little indication of the main direction of the thrust; it might be aimed at Bloemfontein, it could be directed to take Magersfontein from the rear, or it could be to relieve Kimberley.

The only Boer force in the area was commanded by Christiaan de Wet, who reached Waterval Drift, on the Riet

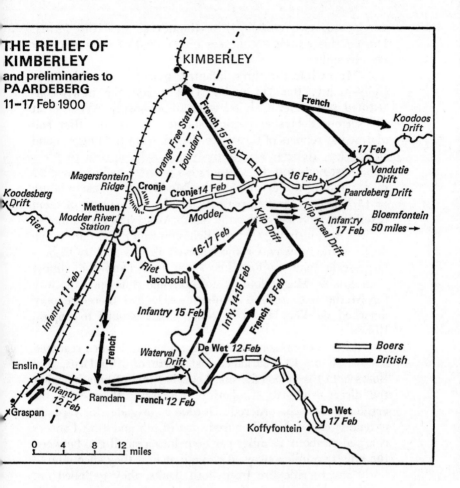

THE RELIEF OF
KIMBERLEY
and preliminaries to
PAARDEBERG
11–17 Feb 1900

KIMBERLEY

French

Koodoos
Drift

Orange Free State boundary

French 15 Feb

17 Feb

Vendutie
Drift

Magersfontein
Ridge

Cronje

Cronje 14 Feb

16 Feb

Paardeberg Drift

Koodesberg
Drift

Methuen
Modder River
Station

Modder

Klip Drift

Klip Kraal Drift

Infantry
17 Feb

Bloemfontein
50 miles →

Riet

16-17 Feb

Riet
Jacobsdal

Infty. 14-15 Feb

French 13 Feb

Infantry 11 Feb

French

Infantry 15 Feb

Waterval
Drift

De Wet 12 Feb

Boers

British

Enslin

Infantry
12 Feb

Ramdam

French 12 Feb

De Wet
17 Feb

Graspan

Koffyfontein

0   4   8   12
miles

River, just before the British cavalry. On 12 February
French edged his way round these Boer positions to cross the
river a few miles further east. Later that day, de Wet pulled
back and was lost sight of by the British who began the
laborious task of getting their wagons through the steep and
narrow drifts. On 13 February the cavalry set out on their
second bound for the Modder where they gained, almost

unopposed, two crossings, at Rondevaal and Klip Drifts. During this march 500 horses either died of exhaustion or became unfit.

Meanwhile the three infantry divisions, the 6th under Kelly-Kenny, the 7th under Tucker and the newly-constituted 9th under Colvile, were all advancing. Worried at the serious delays in getting supplies across the Riet and alarmed at reports of threats to French from the Boers round Kimberley, Roberts saw Kelly-Kenny, who agreed to press on almost non-stop. In 23 hours his infantry had marched 27 miles, joining the cavalry on the Modder in the early hours of 15 February—a fine performance by men, many of them reservists, who had arrived in South Africa less than a month earlier. Still insisting that the British would never dare move far from the railway, Cronje believed all this activity to be a large-scale feint to lure his 7,000 men from the almost impregnable Magersfontein defences and thus open the way for Methuen to relieve Kimberley. He had therefore only detached de Wet and two other small groups to oppose Roberts.

After reorganizing and resting his men, French resumed his march on 15 February. Just north of Klip Drift, 800 Boers held the sides of a small curving line of hills blocking the direct route to Kimberley. Engaging them with his artillery, French ordered Gordon's brigade forward in extended order. Nine hundred men of 9th and 16th Lancers charged at about 14 miles per hour into a small gap between the hills two miles away. Although at first they encountered fairly severe rifle fire from both flanks, they galloped on, raising a huge cloud of dust which soon enveloped their progress. Broadwood's brigade, 1,500 strong, followed about half a mile behind. As Gordon's brigade broke through the gap, the Boers fled from this massed cavalry attack. With only two killed and 17 wounded, French had daringly broken through to Kimberley which, after a brief skirmish *en route*, he entered that evening. During its 124 days' siege, 35 soldiers and five civilians had been killed and 99 soldiers and

24 civilians wounded, but the toll from disease was much heavier.

On 15 February the British suffered their first reverse. With about 1,000 men and a few guns, Christiaan de Wet lurked behind, forgotten by the soldiers toiling to pass supplies across the Riet. Early in the morning he struck at a convoy of 170 oxen and mule wagons whose 1,600 draught oxen and 500 slaughter cattle were scattered grazing on the veld; they were guarded by less than 500 unsuspecting soldiers. Within a few hours de Wet had destroyed or dispersed nearly all the oxen. British detachments, urgently sent back to reinforce those trying to save the wagons, were too weak for the task. To regain and remove the wagons would have meant detaching a sizeable force for several days, therefore Roberts decided to abandon the four days' rations for the army and the valuable medical equipment, but so badly handled was this affair that the wagons were not destroyed. De Wet was, however, diverted for the next crucial two days in transporting his booty and thus took no interest in Cronje's plight.

On the night of 15 February Cronje felt compelled to leave Magersfontein. He chose to go straight for Bloemfontein 90 miles away, thereby taking the most perilous route open to him, because he was moving at right angles to the line of Roberts' advance. Despite the Boers' problems in uprooting themselves, Methuen failed to notice their departure, but, early on 16 February, Hannay's Mounted Infantry, patrolling north of Klip Drift, spotted their huge convoy moving parallel with the Modder. As it slowly surged eastwards, the Mounted Infantry and the men of the 6th Division ineffectively attacked this great prize, but were only able to slow down its progress. Although at first not unduly perturbed, Cronje was faced with two main difficulties. He had to outdistance the British and had to find and hold drifts to cross from the north to the south bank of the Modder, swollen by recent rain. He could reasonably expect help from Ferreira's 2,000 men who slipped away from Kimberley and were, on 17 February, about 15 miles north of him. In addition, he could assume that not only would de Wet soon come to his aid from the south, but also that Steyn in Bloemfontein would assist him by dispatching troops from other fronts. Cronje was, however, greatly handicapped by a shortage of horses; many of the burghers had brought them home, there being no need for them at Magersfontein. He was also burdened by large numbers of women, children and wagons, yet he refused to abandon these hindrances to his mobility.

To halt Cronje, the British had to switch as many of French's cavalry as possible back from Kimberley to the Modder beyond Paardeberg. Very late on 16 February simultaneous orders reached French from Roberts and Kitchener, the latter specifying that his objective should be Koodoos Drift. From his scattered and exhausted horsemen, the only brigade he could muster was Broadwood's. Before dawn on 17 February, French personally led these 1,500 troops with 12 guns, on an epic 30-mile march. On the way they bumped into Ferreira's men, who took fright and withdrew northwards, taking almost no part in the subsequent fighting. (Ferreira was accidentally killed on the night of 18 February, leaving this force leaderless.) By 10.15 hours, French caught up with Cronje who, after a night march, was just starting to cross the Modder at Vendutie Drift, between Paardeberg and Koodoos Drift. By 11.30 hours Royal Horse Artillery batteries were firing at less than 2,500 yards into the Boer laager and, coming from this unexpected quarter, these shells created panic and havoc, especially among the wagon teams. For the remainder of 17 February French's troops harassed the Boers who now began to dig in along the river bed.

It now seemed possible that the British could destroy Cronje's army, but time was short. On 17 February, the crucial day, Roberts fell ill, and temporarily and partially vested command in Kitchener who was accompanying 6 Division. Tactlessly, Kitchener had anyhow been behaving more and more as if he were the Commander-in-Chief, rather than Roberts' Chief-of-Staff and mouthpiece. One thing was, however, becoming clear: Roberts, and even more Kitchener, were passionately concerned with the urgency of bringing Cronje's force to bay. On the other hand, most of the division and brigade commanders took a more phlegmatic approach, being anxious to avoid heavy casualties. The delicate situation of overall command was aggravated because Kitchener, a Major-General, was junior to all Divisional Commanders who were Lieutenant-Generals. Kitchener's position was made more unsatisfactory because as a detached Chief-of-Staff, he had no staff to obtain up-to-date information, to draw up proper plans and to transmit his orders in a less excitable and more intelligible form than these were given out during the heat of the battle on 18 February. Yet for all his mistakes, Kitchener did shoulder the responsibility of directing the battle of Paardeberg and, employing all the forces at his disposal, cornered Cronje.

To return to the progress of the main British force, the inexperienced Mounted Infantry soon lost contact with Cronje. The 6th Division spent 17 February marching eastwards from Klip Kraal Drift along the south bank of the Modder and by nightfall they had reached Signal Hill where, although unaware of it, they were a mere mile south-west of the Boer positions. Here they were joined by the 9th Division, which had hastened from near Jacobsdal; of its reconstituted Highland Brigade, the German Staff History wrote, 'In spite of short rations and the great heat they had marched nearly 31 miles in less than 24 hours, a performance . . . further enhanced by the fact that there were very few stragglers.' The other brigade covered 66 miles in five days, mostly at night.

During the night of 17/18 February Cronje refused pleas from Ferreira, and others amongst his own forces, to break out, taking only his fighting troops. The old man could not discard the tradition, established in native wars, that women and children must never be left to their fate;

nevertheless that night about 400 burghers disobeyed him and escaped. The Boer positions were now spread along four miles, with Vendutie Drift roughly in the centre. They were of great natural strength, being in a gorge of the Modder which is here about 80 yards across. In the scrub, and in many little dry watercourses on the northern bank, the Boers dug small, very narrow, deep trenches and also began tunnelling into the soft 40-feet-high cliffs. All these well-hidden positions were almost iupervious to shell fire.

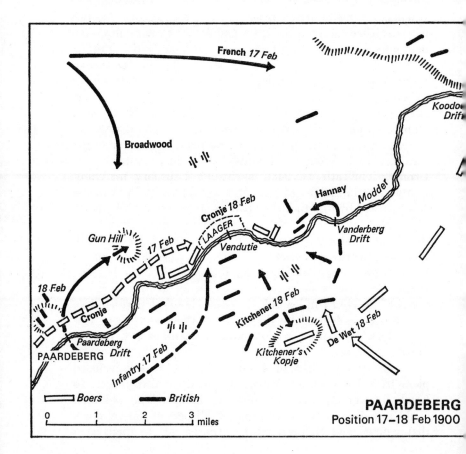

French *17 Feb*

Broadwood

Koodoo Drift

Hannay   Modder

Cronje *18 Feb*
Gun Hill   LAAGER
    17 Feb   Vendutie   Vanderberg
Drift

18 Feb
Cronje

Kitchener *18 Feb*

Paardeberg
PAARDEBERG   Drift   De Wet *18 Feb*

Infantry *17 Feb*   Kitchener's
Kopje

▭ *Boers*   ▬ *British*

0   1   2   3   miles

PAARDEBERG
Position 17–18 Feb 1900

Kitchener determined to storm Cronje's defences before the Boers had had time to dig in too thoroughly, and planned to do this by simultaneous attacks from the south, the east and the west. But both Kelly-Kenny (the most senior officer) and Colvile favoured the less immediately expensive policy of investing Cronje, starving and shelling him into surrender. Although Kitchener on 18 February imposed his plan, he had not worked it out carefully nor did he meet the two Divisional Commanders to explain beforehand his exact purpose. As a result the day's fighting was uncoordinated and confused and impeded by the increasingly lukewarm support of his superior subordinates and their brigade commanders, who not only resented Kitchener's haughty and vague orders that were frequently not transmitted through the correct channels, but also became incensed at the severe losses suffered by their troops.

On 18 February Kitchener's main thrust was directed from the south bank against the two miles of Boer positions downstream from Vendutie Drift. These attacks were pressed home with great bravery, both brigade commanders being wounded, but lack of cover and determined resistance halted most of the troops, either at or just short of the river. As in earlier battles against a river line, this type of head-on offensive was halted, with the soldiers pinned down till dark.

Kitchener also planned an ambitious pincer movement. This was to be launched from the east and the west against the Boer positions on the north bank of the Modder, and, for a short time, the western thrust looked promising. Some Highlanders managed to cross about a mile upstream from Paardeberg Drift, advancing some distance unsupported, before being held up by fire from a deep donga. Unknown to them, Smith-Dorrien's brigade was also crossing the river, and his account of events, though biased, reflects many senior officers' attitude towards Kitchener's conduct of this battle. When questioning Kitchener's messenger as to where to cross, General Smith-Dorrien was told, ' "The river is in flood and as far as I have heard, Paardeberg Drift, the only one available, is unfordable; but Lord Kitchener, knowing

your resourcefulness, feels sure you will get across somehow . . ." ' He concluded, 'The only order I had received was
the one to establish my Brigade on the north side of the river
and I could get neither instructions nor information from
anyone.' With the Canadian battalion, the first to see action
under that country's flag, his brigade made some progress
eastwards, but they were then too far from the river bank to
link up immediately with the Highlanders. Smith-Dorrien
concentrated his main effort on capturing Gun Hill which
dominated the Boer positions, and his guns joined those
south of the river in bombarding Cronje's laager where many
wagons were destroyed. Finally, on this western flank, the
troops were reinforced that evening and made a spirited
charge to try to gain the deep donga, the key to the Boer
strongpoints on this bank. If Smith-Dorrien's 1,000 infantry
had also taken part they might have succeeded, but he knew
nothing of this attack until he saw the troops charging, when
it was too late.

The most dramatic series of events occurred in trying to
carry out the pincer movement on the eastern flank. Before
sunrise, Kitchener sent off most of Hannay's Mounted
Infantry to capture a drift across the Modder in preparation
for a joint attack with Stephenson's brigade, but neither
commander then knew that they were supposed to support
each other in attacking Cronje from the east. *En route*,
Hannay wisely detached about 400 men to occupy a 300-foot
hill (later called Kitchener's Kopje), three miles south of
Cronje's laager, which dominates the surrounding area. He
then went on to seize Vanderberg Drift, linking up with
French whose forces were, however, too exhausted to play a
significant part. Meanwhile, at about 08.00 hours, from the
low hills near Kitchener's Kopje, 300 Boers and two guns
started to fire on Hannay's men from the rear, delaying his
crossing. To meet this threat, Stephenson deployed his men
and with a battery of guns silenced the Boers. By 11.00 hours
the attacks from the south and west had obviously failed and
the excited Kitchener galloped across to get the delayed

9   A Cape cart captured at Cronje's laager. These light, very mobile vehicles were extensively used by the Boer commanders, particularly President Steyn. The drawing is by Captain Leger.

10   The march to Bloemfontein: the 1st Essex bivouacking at Driefontein, March, 1900.

11　Hauling a 4.7 in. Naval gun into position before the Battle of Colenso.

12　The Natal Campaign: engineers constructing a pontoon bridge across the Tugela on the way to Ladysmith.

13   Joubert (*seated, centre*) and his staff at breakfast during the Siege of Ladysmith; his son is on his immediate left.

14   The abortive peace conference at Middelburg in Transvaal on 28 February, 1901. (*Front row, left to right*) de Wet, Botha, Lord Kitchener, and Major-General Sir Bruce Hamilton; Colonel Henderson is standing behind de Wet. The British are wearing black armbands in memory of Queen Victoria.

15 October, 1900: Lord Roberts and his staff at Pretoria. Colonel Rawlinson is on the extreme left.

eastern thrust into motion. During a violent thunderstorm, Hannay had collected most of his scattered troops and crossed to the northern bank. On the southern bank Stephenson was now also halted and, by 14.00 hours, this attack ended. Kitchener was still determined to attempt the pincer movement and Stephenson was given fresh orders to cross to the northern bank to make a concerted attack with Hannay, who received the following injunction from Kitchener: 'The laager must be rushed at all costs. Try and carry Stephenson's brigade with you. But if they cannot go the mounted infantry should do it. Gallop up if necessary and fire into the laager.' During the last ten days Hannay had been subject to stresses and strains which had now become intolerable. He had been given command of six regiments of mounted infantry, most of whom had been hurriedly formed a few weeks earlier by taking a company from various battalions, and some of these men had never been on horseback before. Too untrained to accompany French, his brigade could hardly keep up with the infantry, let alone perform cavalry duties, but having the only mounted troops, Kitchener had ruthlessly urged Hannay on. Now feeling desperate, Hannay led some of his men over the open ground in a suicidal charge against the laager, and was shot to pieces. Later that afternoon, on the eastern flank, Stephenson and a few of the mounted infantry advanced along the north bank of the river, but as on the western flank, this attack lost momentum when it reached the Boer defences, and ground to a halt.

While these final British efforts were being made, de Wet with 600 men suddenly appeared, having ridden up at full speed from Koffyfontein 40 miles to the south. He seized the lightly held Kitchener's Kopje and began firing into British gun positions and wagon parks from the rear. Troops were hurriedly diverted to recapture this dominant feature, but failed to do so by nightfall. Thus this day ended somewhat inconclusively. Although Kitchener had thrown in piecemeal all the forces at his disposal, they had not managed to storm Cronje's stronghold, but the Boers were so battered that only a handful of determined men broke out to join de Wet.

By 19 February Roberts had recovered sufficiently to take over at Paardeberg, and found the senior officers were appalled by the casualties. Despite the imminent arrival of Tucker's 7th Division and other reinforcements, they adamantly opposed Kitchener's plan for another assault against Cronje, now penned into two miles of the river bed and bank. The steam had now gone out of this offensive and, in very hot weather, the British settled down to a mixture of bombardment and nibbling night attacks which steadily contracted Cronje's positions. Simultaneously, attempts were made to dislodge de Wet, whose force had grown to 1,500 men. He was eventually driven off Kitchener's Kopje on 21 February and escaped without having made a serious effort to break through the British lines to rescue Cronje! Now abandoned, Cronje surrendered on 27 February, which was, ironically, Majuba Day. It was also an historic day for Canada because the final attack on the laager was spearheaded by the Royal Canadian Regiment who thereby won the first of many battle honours gained by their army.

At Paardeberg the Boers lost about 4,250 soldiers (nearly 10% of their field fighting force); 2,700 Transvaalers and 1,400 Free Staters were taken prisoner, the number killed being only 117. Despite the loss of 300 killed and 1,000 wounded (nearly all on the first day), the British gained their first decisive victory of the campaign. The Boer leaders had to admit that, short of a miracle, no hope now remained of defeating their enemy by conventional methods, but the feasibility of waging a widespread and prolonged guerrilla war was not yet perceived. On the Cape Colony–Orange Free State front, the collapse of Boer morale was immediately apparent, and an almost complete withdrawal took place across the Orange River by men who wished to protect their homes and defend Bloemfontein. Acting under Roberts' orders to keep casualties to the minimum, neither Gatacre nor Clements tried to pursue these Boers who mostly escaped intact with their equipment.

CHAPTER EIGHT

The Final Battle for Ladysmith

'My general was shot in the water bottle, so you can imagine what it was like for us.'

> *General Lyttelton's batman on the fighting at*
> *Wynne Hill.*

On 12 February, the same day as Roberts' offensive started, fighting on the Natal front was resumed. With 25,000 men, Buller began his fourth attempt to relieve Ladysmith and succeeded in doing so on 28 February. His hesitant, muddled, and often expensive series of attacks can be divided into three phases, the first lasting from 12 to 19 February. After a three-day pause, imposed by Buller because of the heat, Dundonald's locally recruited mounted troops made a daring advance. Largely on their own initiative, on 17 February they drove the Boers from their dominating positions on Cingolo Mountain. Lyttelton's 2nd Division followed up this important breakthrough and both Monte Cristo and Green Hill were captured the next day, while on 19 February the Boers evacuated Hlangwane, the key to the Tugela crossing places. But Buller held Lyttelton's troops back from pursuing the 2,000 Boers, who fled in disorder across the Tugela; an excellent opportunity to obtain a victory was lost by default. The British had now cleared the whole eastern bank of the Tugela, northwards from Colenso, at the cost of 25 killed and 280 wounded.

Reitz has described the pandemonium on 18–19 February. 'Hundreds of men were leaving the new line that had been formed in the hills behind the abandoned trenches . . . Up to now, the prevailing note in Natal had been one of confidence in an early peace, but, almost in a night and without apparent cause, a wave of pessimism had set in.' Even Botha temporarily lost heart, asking Kruger's permission to withdraw beyond Ladysmith. The old President sternly refused, justifying his decision with a long telegram studded with Biblical quotations; including 'Stand fast in faith to fight, and you shall be convinced that the Lord shall arise and scatter his enemies. Our faith is now at its utmost test'. Although rumours of Cronje's calamitous predicament were circulating, Botha's spirits revived and, by delaying his next move for two days, Buller almost answered Kruger's prayers.

The second phase of the advance lasted from 20 to 25 February. Buller decided the only feasible place to cross the Tugela was just north of Colenso where he ordered the pontoon bridge to be constructed. On 21 February he optimistically heliographed White, 'I think that there is only a rearguard in front of me . . . I hope to be with you tomorrow night.' By 22 February most of both Warren's and Lyttelton's divisions (15 battalions and 40 guns) were crammed into a narrow strip of ground by the river which was everywhere overlooked by hills. At the northern end of this small flat area, the road and railway are squeezed together by a group of hills that come down almost to the Tugela, their false crests proving excellent defensive positions. On these and other encircling hills Botha assembled about 5,000 men. From 22 to 24 February the British troops fought some of the costliest battles of the whole war. To begin with, Wynne's brigade tried to storm the hills that dominate the route to Ladysmith. In spite of reinforcements and strong artillery support, the Boers forced the British infantry to abandon their gallant attempts on 23 February, and the main obstacle, Wynne's Hill as it came to be called, continued to block any advance. Hart's Irish brigade

managed to circumvent it by scrambling along the river bed
and attacking Terrace Hill, the next major obstruction. But
the same story was repeated. The whole offensive came to a
halt, with the Boer enfilading fire harassing the British
troops who were closely packed. On 25 February, a Sunday,
a ceasefire was arranged to collect the wounded and the dead
from the slopes of the hills. The British lost 212 killed and
nearly 1,200 wounded and missing in the four days' fighting,
and had little to show for it.

The last phase of this offensive began on 26 February
when the pontoon bridge was dismantled and then re-erected
two miles downstream. On 27 February Buller, having carefully explained his plans to his commanders, for the first
time employed all his forces in a well-concerted attack. On
the southern flank, Lyttelton's 2nd Division was detailed to
hold the Boers in their positions and give whatever other
assistance was possible. Three brigades of Warren's 5th
Division were to cross the Tugela by the newly erected
pontoon bridge and fan out to attack on a wide front.
Barton's brigade was to lead the way by capturing Pieter's
Hill, the most northerly objective. Walter Kitchener's*
brigade was to follow and seize Railway Hill and finally
Norcott was directed to take Terrace Hill. From across the
Tugela, 91 guns, of various sizes (including a 6 in. naval
gun, four 4·7 in. naval guns and four 5 in. guns) began a
bombardment, providing heavy and accurate concentrations
of very close support-fire for the infantry. By 27 February
the British had blasted a gap through the Boer defences with
a loss of less than 500 men, and the exhausted, demoralized
Boers streamed back. Buller's victory should have been complete. Early on 28 February all the Boer commandos from
the Tugela and Ladysmith began a chaotic retreat which
neither Botha nor President Kruger, who came from Pretoria
to intervene, could stem; even Joubert, now a dying man,
fled. As Reitz recalled, 'The plain was covered with a multi-
tude of men, wagons and guns ploughing across the sodden

* Lord Kitchener's brother.

veld in the greatest disorder . . . it seemed as if the bulk of
the transport and artillery would have to be abandoned, for
the mounted men pressed steadily on without concerning
themselves with the convoys. Had the British fired a single
gun at this surging mob everything on wheels would have
fallen into their hands.' The Boers need not have feared.
Buller refused to consider a pursuit, and it was solely by
Dundonald's insistence that Captain Gough's squadron was
allowed to press on to reach Ladysmith on the evening of 28
February, thus ending the 118-day siege. Next day, White
sent out a column from Ladysmith to try to take advantage of
the Boer collapse, but the men were too weak to get far; on
hearing of this action, Buller ordered them to return immediately. Buller now devoted all his resources to bringing
in food, and he excused himself later by saying, 'I had no
doubt from what I saw and from General White's information, that the enemy were in full retreat, and retreating Boers
are very difficult to catch, especially when they have 24 hours
start on you.'

Ladysmith had cost the British about 7,000 casualties,
Buller spending over three months, and fighting four battles
before relieving the town. Once there, Buller frittered away
10 weeks before resuming his advance. He who so desperately
tried to save his troops from danger and discomfort was once
again responsible for prolonging the war by granting the
Boers the chance to rest, regroup and revive.

CHAPTER NINE

The Capture of the Capitals

'The Boer's first concern is for his safety.'
Colonel de Villebois-Mareuil.

'Strolling across the middle of the square, quite alone, was a very small grey-haired gentleman, with extremely broad shoulders and a most unbending back . . . I knew that I was looking at the Queen's greatest subject, the commander who had in the brief space of a month revolutionized the fortunes of the war.'
Winston Churchill, 16 April, 1900, at Bloemfontein.

Early in March the Boer Republics faced a supreme crisis and Kruger rushed to join Steyn. To arrange a negotiated peace settlement, the two Presidents had to prevent their countries from being invaded and conquered. This meant rallying sufficient of their scattered and demoralized forces to repulse Roberts, whose supply lines were stretched. The place the Boers chose for their new stand was Poplar Grove, about 50 miles west of Bloemfontein and 15 miles east of Paardeberg, where de Wet was already occupying one of the series of kopjes that lie either side of the Modder. If this line could be held, it would bar the route to the capital. By 7 March, when Roberts' attack began, de Wet had collected 8,000 men, but they were strung out over a front of nearly 20 miles.

Roberts' plan was to outflank this line in the north with French's cavalry, and then launch two infantry divisions against the main positions so as to drive the Boers into the

93

Modder valley, trapping them as at Paardeberg. This enterprising plan depended for its success not only on precise timing and resolute and energetic leadership on the British side, but also on the willingness of the Boers to stand and fight. None of these essential preconditions was fulfilled and the desultory inconclusive engagement at Poplar Grove was the first of many to take place during the next three months between the advancing British and retreating Boer forces. On 7 March, French was in an uncooperative mood, feeling that his undernourished horses were being expected to make too long a march. He started late and allowed small Boer rearguard parties to delay his progress, while most of the infantry were slow to arrive and not imbued with any sense of alacrity. Nevertheless, de Wet wrote, 'A panic seized my men. Before the English had even got near enough to shell our positions to any purpose, the wild flight began.' Visiting de Wet that morning, Kruger was caught up in this rout, but the elderly top-hatted President escaped in his Cape cart. So half-hearted and cautious was the attack that the Boers lost hardly a man, gun or wagon.

On 10 March Roberts resumed his march on Bloemfontein. He divided his cavalry between his three infantry divisions who moved in echelon. On the left, French commanded the leading column, Roberts himself took the centre one and Tucker the right-hand column. After going about 15 miles, French's advance guard were held up by enemy fire from the most northerly of four kopjes occupied by about 6,000 Boer who were again trying to hold back the British. During the afternoon a fierce little battle developed along this 10-mile line, mainly on Driefontein kopje where de la Rey and a contingent of South African Police put up a resolute defence before being dislodged by Stephenson's brigade. The British lost 438 men, 87 killed, and the Boers over 100 killed. This engagement knocked the heart out of their rank and file and no attempt was made to hold Bloemfontein. French pushed on rapidly and the town was formally surrendered on 13 March and a silk Union Jack, made by Lady

Roberts, was hoisted on the flagstaff opposite the President's house. The citizens of Bloemfontein were surprisingly friendly. Some of the troops went there for a meal, and one commented, 'Bought some bread 1/– per small loaf. First piece of bread for 30 days'.

Many considered that the capture of Bloemfontein was tantamount to the war ending, and all that now remained was to march peacefully 300 miles to Pretoria, showing the Transvaalers that they were also defeated. Roberts trustingly released most of the Boer prisoners who promised not to fight again and who handed in one rifle, usually their oldest, the new Mauser or Martini-Henry being hidden. Although the Boers appeared defeated, the British were none too favourably placed. With already depleted ranks, reinforcements had to be brought up before the army could advance again, and it badly needed new equipment, especially boots. Equally serious were the heavy losses in horses, and the poor condition of those which had survived. Time was also needed to switch the supply depot from Cape Town to Port Elizabeth thereby shortening the supply line by about 300 miles. But not until the end of March were trains running across the Orange River at Norval's Pont, while at Bethulie each truck had to be man-handled over the temporary crossing. The most critical problem was, however, the severe outbreak of typhoid (enteric fever) in which the sufferings of the thousands of stricken men were temporarily reminiscent of the Crimea. On 28 April *The Times* correspondent reported that, 'men were dying like flies for want of adequate attention . . . with only a blanket and a thin waterproof sheet . . . with no beds, no milk and hardly any medicines . . . with only a few private soldiers to act as "orderlies".' So scarce were hospital beds that bell tents, supposed to accommodate six to eight, were crammed with the typhoid cases. 'Equipment of all kinds,' he continued, 'except for the sick, had been moving up during this leisurely time' (the seven weeks' halt at Bloemfontein).

During this period less than 6,000 Boers held scattered positions round Ladysmith, but Buller with 45,000 soldiers made no move. Instead he wrote to Roberts about future plans and Roberts tacitly condoned Buller's inaction. Roberts was more enterprising and his troops soon linked up with Gatacre and Clements, who had advanced across the Orange River. At first, British detachments roamed confidently around the southern Orange Free State visiting small towns where they showed the flag, which was normally hauled down directly they departed. Four isolated garrisons were installed, one of the largest being Broadwood's with 1,700 men at Thabanchu, 40 miles east of the capital.

Taking advantage of this lull, the Boers regrouped. They were spurred on by President Steyn and some of the younger leaders who were preparing to wage guerrilla warfare. The most forceful figure was Christiaan de Wet who planned to destroy the Bloemfontein waterworks, near Sannah's Post, guarded by 200 Mounted Infantry. On 31 March, he led 1,600 men there, and when Broadwood's unsuspecting column, retiring from Thabanchu to Bloemfontein, crossed his path, he ambushed it at Sannah's Post, taking over 400 prisoners, killing and wounding 170, capturing seven of the twelve guns and 83 of the 92 wagons. Although a mere 20 miles away, relief columns of superior numbers, coming from Bloemfontein, failed to give Broadwood any effective assistance and de Wet escaped with his booty. The loss of the waterworks further worsened the typhoid epidemic.

On 4 April near Dewetsdorp, de Wet struck at another of the isolated garrisons whose troops were trying to march to safety. In this case, after a stand of less than a day and with 10 killed and 35 wounded, de Wet compelled 546 Regular soldiers to surrender. The humiliation was aggravated by Gatacre being close at hand and not marching to the rescue; Roberts was so incensed that he dismissed Gatacre. De Wet summarized his tactics: 'This war demanded *rapidity of action* more than anything else. We had to be quick at fighting, quick at reconnoitring, quick (if it became necessary) at flying!' But later in April, de Wet had a setback which demonstrated one of the major limitations which confronts every guerrilla force. Near Wepener, on the Basuto border, with 5,000 men, he besieged the garrison of 1,900 soldiers, mainly South Africans, for sixteen days, but they stood firm. The burghers would not face the losses needed to storm these positions and had to flee when the relieving force appeared. De Wet wrote about these local opponents: 'Although I never took it amiss if a colonist of Natal or Cape Colony was unwilling to fight with us against England, yet I admit that it vexed me greatly to think that some of these colonists, for the sake of a paltry five shillings a day should be ready to shoot down their own countrymen.' From now onwards the bitter emotions of civil war were more often stirred up, especially when Boers, including later Christiaan de Wet's brother Piet, joined the British, becoming 'hands uppers'.

As the guerrilla war tentatively started, the conventional war reached its climax. On 3 May the British launched their supposedly final offensive. With 44,000 soldiers, nearly

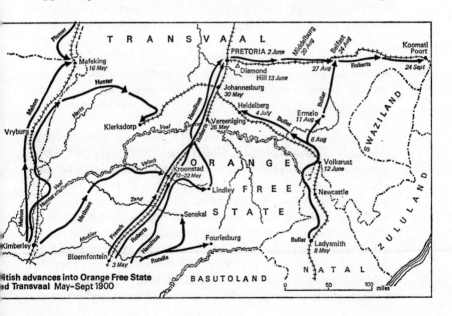

British advances into Orange Free State and Transvaal May–Sept 1900

11,000 horses, 22,000 mules drawing 5,500 carts, and 40,000 oxen pulling 2,500 wagons, each with its native driver, and supported by 120 guns and fourteen 1 pounder Maxim-Vickers, Roberts' large army set out from Bloemfontein for Pretoria. Roberts commanded the main body which moved up both sides of the railway, French's cavalry division was west of the line, and Pole-Carew's 11th Division and Tucker's 7th Division, supported by Mounted Infantry regiments, marched east of the railway. Acting as a semi-independent force, on the eastern flank, Hamilton's Mounted Infantry Division, strengthened by a cavalry brigade and backed by Colville's 9th Division, led the offensive. The British were opposed by about 15,000 Boers. The Transvaalers were under Botha and de la Rey, while the Free Staters were commanded by de Wet who temporarily abandoned his guerrilla activities to try to check this massive invasion. Although they intended to hold the Zand and Valsch river lines, the Boers could not withstand Roberts' army, and fell steadily back. On 12 May the British were compelled to stop at Kroonstad having covered 130 miles. The railway had to be repaired to permit supplies to come forward; and while the cavalry were exhausted, nearly 1,000 of their 6,000 horses having died, many were still soft after their long sea voyage (some had just come from the Argentine) and were not acclimatized to work at 4,500 feet in extremes of cold and heat.

During this pause, news was received that Colonel Mahon's flying column, which had been specially constituted for this operation, had joined Plumer's force and relieved Mafeking on 16 May. Just before its relief, the town had been in some danger when Kruger's grandson, Eloff, broke in with a small determined group, but they were checked, and surrendered. Mahon's combined force also drove off de le Rey and 2,000 Boers. Mafeking's relief sparked off paroxysms of rejoicing throughout Britain and the Empire. Baden-Powell had become a national hero, epitomizing the virtues of humour, doggedness, resourcefulness and courage.

During the 217 days of siege the casualties were 67 men killed and 135 wounded or missing.

On 8 May Buller's forces set out from Ladysmith heading north for Laing's Nek and the Transvaal. (It would have been far better if Roberts had insisted that the Natal army go westwards, through the easier Van Reenen's Pass into the Orange Free State from whence they could have given more direct help to the main British advance.) Buller reached Newcastle fairly rapidly, but from then onwards his progress was snail-like. Between 19 May and 12 June he only managed 20 miles, having taken one of the most difficult routes possible to circumvent Laing's Nek and Majuba Hill, where the Boers resisted fiercely. On 12 June, Buller was just over the Transvaal border and the last invader had been ejected from Natal.

On 22 May Roberts' forces resumed their advance from Kroonstad, crossing the Vaal River on 26 May when they entered Transvaal. On 30 May, after a sharp engagement at Doorn Kop just south of the city, Johannesburg surrendered, its mines undamaged. On 2 June Kruger left Pretoria and on the 5th Roberts entered the capital after a western flanking move. This enabled most of the Boer officials, taking their gold, to escape by rail, but over 3,000 British prisoners of war were released before the Boers could move them. 13,800 foot soldiers had covered 300 miles in 34 days, mainly over trackless country, on very short rations, in mid-winter and with a wastage rate of less than 4%. The cavalry fared worse, poor quality remounts and bad horse-management having reduced their numbers heavily; nevertheless, the survivors had covered 380 miles. The total battle casualties were light, 109 killed, 479 wounded and missing, but of the 38,000 who set out from Bloemfontein only about 26,000 actually reached Pretoria. Some troops were left to garrison important places *en route*, others fell out through sickness. Many also dropped out with incapacitated horses and, with the cavalry so depleted, Roberts' weary army was sadly lacking in mobility.

About 12 miles east of Pretoria, the Boers made their final coordinated attempt to stop the British by a conventional stand. To prevent being outflanked, they occupied a 25-mile front along a group of steep broken hills through the centre of which ran the Delagoa Bay railway. On 11 June French's cavalry was soon pinned down at the northern end by de la Rey's men, who held a fortress-like stronghold. Further south, round Diamond Hill, Ian Hamilton's troops made some progress before they too were halted. They were reinforced the next day, when heavy, but inconclusive fighting continued. On 13 June the Boers melted away, but their adversaries were too weak to pursue them and anyhow there seemed little reason for so doing. A Member of Parliament serving with the Dorset Yeomanry summed up the general feeling when he wrote home, 'All say the war is virtually over'.

CHAPTER TEN

The First Phase of the Guerrilla Campaign June–September, 1900

'About a dozen other Generals were sent in all directions, some with flying columns, others to repress
specific threatening small bodies of the enemy, others to
garrison certain towns, and all detached from their
regular commands . . . the Chief [Roberts] had to upset
his main plans and carry out fresh ones at a moment's
notice.'

Smith-Dorrien, writing of July, 1900

'How England utterly under-estimated the determination of the Boers, subsequent events have plainly
proved. It is equally plain that we ourselves did not
know the strength of our resolution, when one takes
into account the pessimism and despair that weighed us
down in those dark days.'

Ben Viljoen, My Reminiscences.

The early part of June was a crucial period for the Boer
cause. After the fall of Pretoria, most of the Transvaalers
went home and some of their leaders were ready to sue for
peace, considering that the war was irretrievably lost. They
were dissuaded mainly by the determination of the Free
Staters who from now onwards represented the more
intransigent element. To explain how this crisis between the
two allies was resolved, it is necessary to return to earlier
events. Between 30 May and 7 June the Free State forces

101

gained three spectacular successes; first they induced Spragge with 500 Yeomanry to surrender near Lindley; four days later they captured a large convoy and its escort near Heilbron; and finally de Wet descended on the Central Railway, the 1,000-mile lifeline of the British Army, cutting it in three places and destroying the bridge over the Rhenoster River. Together with losses in various other skirmishes, the British suffered over 1,500 casualties in under ten days, far more than during their epic march to Pretoria.

Early in June the Transvaal leaders gathered together for a council of war in a distillery just outside Pretoria. At first they could see little hope for the future. Botha was just about to leave to negotiate with Roberts, and the terms would have been unconditional surrender, when suddenly these victories were announced. Realizing the vulnerability of the British to such guerrilla tactics, the Transvaalers' spirits immediately revived, and although they had failed at Diamond Hill, this did not deter them from starting to reorganize their forces. With hindsight, the main reasons can now be seen which convinced so many Boers that they could still hope to compel Britain to sue for peace. In the first place, most of the original and discredited leaders had disappeared from the scene, Cronje had been captured, Joubert had died, Martin Prinsloo was to surrender at Brandwater Basin in July and Kruger, a broken man, finally left for Holland in September. They were replaced by a remarkably able group of men, Christiaan de Wet, Judge Hertzog and Kritzinger in Orange Free State, and in Transvaal Louis Botha, Koos de la Rey and Ben Viljoen, who had all proved themselves to be outstanding in battle. The implacable President Steyn contributed a measure of political continuity, while Jan Smuts was emerging as a military figure of the first rank. These men were dedicated to the Boer cause and could inspire their followers to endure terrible hardships; they were to astound the British, and indeed the whole world.

16, 17 and 18 Kitchener's young column commanders who distinguished themselves in this campaign and became senior Army commanders in the First World War. Lt-Colonel D. Haig (*left*), Colonel E. H. H. Allenby (*below left*) and Lt-Colonel H. Plumer (*below right*).

19   A British column crossing Kaffir Spruit; note the mule cart in the foreground and the length of the column stretching behind.

20   Kritzinger's commando in Cape Colony saddling up in December, 1900.

Surveying the prospects for the future, the new Boer commanders could congratulate themselves on never having been decisively defeated. In the many battles and skirmishes fought between October, 1899, and June, 1900, their losses had been light, perhaps 1,500 men killed in action and probably about 10% of these had been foreign volunteers. Admittedly tens of thousands of burghers had been captured or had deserted or returned home, but for the Boer cause this was no bad thing. It had painlessly disposed of the faint-hearted, while it was soon found that the less resolute, after a period of rest, could be rallied, and, when the occasion arose, would operate from their own districts. By August the British were beginning to burn the farms of Boers who took up arms again and this policy of destruction converted moderates into hard-core fighters; both Fuller and Smuts later considered farm-burning was counter-productive and may even have lengthened the war. As this scorched-earth policy gathered momentum, it particularly incensed the women who became, in Ian Hamilton's opinion, even more 'bitter and irreconcilable' opponents of British rule. The guerrilla war turned almost into a religious crusade, but, it must be emphasized, without the wholesale atrocities that normally characterize such conflicts.

The Boers also cherished an unshakeable illusion that they could induce the countries sympathetic to their cause to come to their rescue and stop Transvaal and Orange Free State being added to the British Empire. For some months, a three-man mission had been visiting the capitals of the western world, but in Washington, Berlin, Paris and St Petersburg they met the same negative response. World opinion was almost universally favourable to the Boers, and the Dutch and French governments would have liked to make some practical gestures of support. But the British, with their formidable navy, were too powerful to be worth antagonizing over a region of Africa where these countries had no ready means of intervention. Moreover, some of their citizens had large stakes in the Rand gold mines whose security was

5

bound to be jeopardized by any prolongation of this war. Thus in their quest for outside assistance, the Boers drew a blank. Finally the Boer leaders pinned great hopes on British public opinion. They reasoned that a combination of war-weariness and expense would make this conflict increasingly unpopular, that the Conservatives would be overthrown and the Liberals returned to power on the pledge of ending the war. Lloyd George and other Liberals and Socialists advocated this policy and stormy meetings were held through-out Britain. But in the Khaki election of October, 1900, the Conservatives were comfortably re-elected. The tenacious and self-confident patriotism of the great bulk of the British people prevailed and, even in this increasingly pointless war, they were determined on victory. Nevertheless, the Boer vision of undermining their adversary's will-power by anti-war propaganda on the home front was to pioneer a new method of conducting war which, under different circum-stances, was to succeed in the United States of America during the Vietnam War.

A guerrilla war tends to be a confused and confusing affair. The initiative is normally taken by the guerrillas, whose operations are characteristically unexpected and with-out much centralized direction. This sporadic, fragmentary type of war is difficult to describe and follow, because no proper chronological pattern exists to give it the coherence of the more formalized conventional war. Between June, 1900, and the end of May, 1902, spasmodic fighting flared up in nearly all parts of Transvaal, most of Orange Free State, as well as in many parts of Cape Colony. Across nearly 150,000 square miles, dozens of wandering groups of Boers, normally 50–200 strong and never more than about 25,000 men in all actually in the field, fought over 200,000 British soldiers. Although the majority of the British were in static posts protecting vulnerable lines of communication, up to 75,000 eventually became mobile, being formed into columns of 1,000–5,000 troops who spent much of their time pursuing their elusive opponents. It took more than a year before

Kitchener's blockhouse system, to protect the railways, imposed some kind of pattern on the war. It was even longer before this restrictive measure, together with the scorched-earth policy of farm burning, gave the British decisively the upper hand. With the Boers launching a new type of warfare, little theoretical or practical experience existed from which either side could draw to construct plans or counterplans. Inevitably, therefore, both sides sometimes made what now appear to be foolish errors in the conduct of this strange and desultory campaign.

From mid-June to October, 1900, the Boers were mainly concerned with regrouping their forces for this new kind of war. The three major leaders were de la Rey in western and Botha in eastern Transvaal, and de Wet in Orange Free State. Roberts made his first priority the destruction of the Orange Free State forces who were such a menace to the Central Railway. As Ian Hamilton had been injured by falling from his horse, Hunter (of Ladysmith fame) was given command of 18,000 men and advanced southwards from Transvaal at the end of June. A preliminary task was to help Paget who had been besieged for three weeks by de Wet in Lindley, a strategically important small town that had already changed hands seven times during the last fortnight of May! Lindley being quickly relieved, the British pushed on to expel the Free Staters from their temporary capital at Bethlehem. Nearly 7,000 of them now fell back into the remote Brandwater Basin on the Basutoland border where a horseshoe-shaped range of mountains enclosed a fertile tract of country. With few and easily defendable entrances, this appeared to be a safe natural fortress. But with the British already blocking some of the exits and approaching the others, de Wet thought otherwise, and, accompanied by President Steyn, he silently led 2,500 men, four guns and over 400 light wagons through one of the northern passes before Hunter could seal it off. Passing very close to Paget's force on 15 July, de Wet later repulsed minor British attacks and doubled back towards Lindley and escaped the net. The rest

of the Orange Free State forces were supposed to split into
four groups and follow de Wet the next day, but a dispute
arose, which dragged on for a fortnight, as to who was in
command. In the meantime, Hunter's troops wrested two
passes in the north from the Boers and entered this map-less
area. On 27 July, after a prolonged Council of War, the
elderly Prinsloo was elected leader, when it was too late to
make a mass break-out. On 29 July 4,140 of Prinsloo's men
surrendered with three guns, but 1,500 determined Free
Staters slipped out through the rugged, isolated easternmost
pass that was not blocked in time. Although it was a memorable British victory, ranking with Paardeberg, it did
strengthen the new Boer leaders because it also eliminated
some less dedicated fighters.

To return to de Wet and President Steyn. They were
recognized as archetypal foes whose capture or death would
have an immense effect on the Boer cause. As soon as he
could, Roberts switched most of his best forces on what came
to be known as the first de Wet hunt, but the pursuit started
most ineffectively. The lack of any intelligence-gathering
system on the march was highlighted when two British
columns moved parallel to each other unknowingly for three
days, during which time their uncoordinated attacks were
easily repulsed. De Wet, on the other hand, had excellent
subordinates, including Danie Theron whose international
Corps of 200 Scouts (which included Russians, a Bulgar, a
Greek, a Turk and an Algerian Arab) provided a permanent
flow of information which usually enabled de Wet to
anticipate British moves. He therefore had little difficulty in
breaking through the first major barrier, the Central Railway, which he crossed by dividing his forces, Theron's
contingent ambushing a store train in the process. By 25
July de Wet installed himself in a strong position by the
Vaal River, 20 miles south of Potchefstroom. He stayed in
this friendly district skirmishing with the British and raiding
the railway while debating his next move.

By early August 11,000 British troops were assembled

south and 18,000 north of the Vaal, and Roberts sent
Kitchener to take charge of the operation of cornering de
Wet against one of three successive obstacles. With 3,000
men, Methuen guarded the first of these, the Vaal River
crossings, but Kitchener ordered him to the wrong drift. On
6 August de Wet crossed safely into Transvaal, but it was
only by taking a three-mile-long convoy of wagons that he
persuaded the Free Staters to quit their own country. During
the following eight days de Wet urged his men on relent-
lessly, eluding or just out-marching the British who were
always close on his heels. By again splitting his column, giving one part to Theron, de Wet at first convinced Kitchener
that he was going to double back across the Vaal which put
the British off the scent, but instead he swung north heading
for the Gatsrand. This small but steep ridge of hills was the
hide-out for Libenberg's active commando whose many raids
on the Johannesburg–Klerksdorp railway had forced the
British to evacuate Potchefstroom and Klerksdorp. This railway line, the second obstacle, lay at right angles to de Wet's
path, and Smith-Dorrien's experienced brigade was poised to
halt him there. Again faulty information saved him, because
Roberts ordered the unwilling Smith-Dorrien to concentrate
his force to the north of where de Wet crossed the line, which
he did by night, continuing his exhausting march just ahead
of the British. Between de Wet and safety still lay the final
and much greater obstacle, the Megaliesberg. This lofty
range of mountains starts just north of Pretoria and then
extends westwards for over 100 miles with only four passes
through it. De Wet chose Olifant's Nek which Ian Hamilton
was ordered to block, but, wrongly advised about de Wet's
timing, he moved too slowly, arriving after the last Boer
wagons had gone through. Believing that Hamilton was
guarding the entrance to Olifant's Nek, Methuen, who was
catching up on de Wet, veered off to the west to prevent the
Boer column escaping in that direction.

De Wet had escaped and could now relax. He entered
the region dominated by de la Rey whose 7,000 West

Transvaalers had, for the last month, been striking at British units all round the west of Pretoria. Steyn went off to confer with the Transvaal government and, splitting up his forces, de Wet took only 250 men. After some narrow escapes, he returned to his former hide-out by the Vaal, and, at the end of August, he was back, cutting the Central Railway and recruiting more burghers. In less than 50 days, he had traversed 500 miles through a supposedly pacified part of South Africa tying down tens of thousands of British soldiers in a fruitless chase.

The first 'de Wet hunt' vividly demonstrated that the British had not mastered the art of scouting and keeping their quarry under constant observation; their haphazard, small scouting parties were often captured by the Boers who could normally outride them. This chase also revealed the defects of the centralized British command (in all nine columns were employed), whose information was often faulty, as was shown by the orders sent to Methuen and Smith-Dorrien. The system of tight control also tended to under-estimate the speed of events, and thus directions tended to be sent out too late to be effective, as was the case with Hamilton's column. These weaknesses continued to plague the British army for the rest of the campaign. On the credit side, the British proved that they could match the Boer columns when it came to marching. In August, Smith-Dorrien's brigade covered 116 miles in seven days and 245 miles in eighteen days, on only two of which did they rest. Other troops did equally well, one brigade marching for 40 out of 48 hours. Many of the men had no boots and their clothes were in rags, one private summed it up by remarking, ''Ere we are again, mate, off on another blooming trek, 'alf rations and full congratulations.' Finally, de Wet's success in evading the British was partly attributable to the unreserved cooperation of local farmers who provided their fellow countrymen not only with supplies and information, but also sometimes with places from which to snipe at the 'red necks', the Boer nickname for British soldiers.

In eastern Transvaal, the main problem confronting Botha was organizing resistance in a region which comprised all the Transvaal east of the railway line from Vereeniging to Pietersburg. Most of the centre and south of this huge territory is veined with rivers whose valleys and hills afford good cover for guerrillas; the drawback to this sparsely populated area is the fever-ridden low veld along the Crocodile River. President Kruger and the Transvaal government were under Botha's care and installed in railway carriages at Machadodorp about 150 miles east of Pretoria.

After the inconclusive battle of Diamond Hill in June, Roberts might have ended the war if he could have captured the Transvaal government. This feat would have demanded a rapid advance eastwards along the railway to sever the Boers' last link with the outside world. Roberts was diverted from this task for two main reasons, first the exhaustion and depletion of his forces, especially the cavalry, and, secondly, the guerrilla activities of de Wet and de la Rey to the north, south and west of Pretoria; thus for nearly two months Botha remained almost unmolested. But Roberts must partly be blamed for this inactivity because, by mid-June, Buller's advance formations had reached Volksrust, a mere 125 miles south of Machadodorp and Roberts should then have directed him to move northwards, to cut the Delagoa Bay railway (as even Buller himself vaguely suggested), thereby threatening the rear of Botha's forces. Instead, Roberts permitted Buller to continue his leisurely progress along the Natal railway until, on 4 July, his advance guard joined hands with Roberts' forces at Heidelberg.

Early in July Botha went on the offensive. In conjunction with de la Rey's operations north and west of Pretoria, which included the British surrender of 240 men at Zilikiat's Nek, Botha occupied the Tigerspoort Ridge area with 3,000 men, thereby menacing Pretoria from the east. To meet this combination of threats, Roberts postponed his intended offensive eastwards, employing French and Ian Hamilton to safeguard Pretoria which was lightly garrisoned.

Although now desperately short of troops, Roberts still made almost no use of Buller's army.

After Botha's forces were dislodged from the Tiger-spoort district, they returned to near Balmoral and Roberts began an advance eastwards. On 23 July Ian Hamilton's column moved north of the railway, Pole-Carew with the infantry marched along the railway, whilst French's cavalry prepared to outflank the Boers from the south. After three days in which considerable progress was made, Roberts abandoned the operation, partly because he did not wish to risk the cavalry, partly because of the shortage of men and supplies, but mainly because of de la Rey and de Wet's activities. To counter their attacks Ian Hamilton's force was withdrawn. Although Middelburg was taken, none of Buller's forces, now less than 100 miles away, were even now ordered to link up with French, whose outflanking moves were making good progress and who continued to push forward during the next three weeks. At last, Roberts ordered Buller to march northwards to join French. On 7 August 11,000 troops, mainly from 4th Division, now recovered from their privations in the Ladysmith siege, set out from Volksrust northwards, via Ermelo. They met little opposition and, on 15 August, linked up with French's forces about 30 miles south of Belfast. The British were now approaching a 50-mile line of fortified posts held by about 6,000 Boers. These positions lay mainly to the north of the railway by Belfast, and had been chosen by Botha. Most of the Boers who occupied them had grown tired of waiting for the British, so there was, at first, little inclination for any determined resistance, but President Steyn visited many detachments and his enthusiasm, oratory and magnetic personality revived the spirits of the defenders.

After another pause to regroup and bring up supplies, the final offensive of the conventional style warfare began on 27 August. At the outset, an opportunity, albeit a difficult one, still existed of capturing Kruger. French wanted to sweep rapidly round the south to Barberton, and then north to the railway, cutting off the Boer line of retreat. Roberts modified the plan and then Buller postponed it, failing once again to appreciate the high stakes at issue. Thus this offensive degenerated into a laborious and arduous advance, giving the Boers plenty of time to make arrangements for continuing the campaign. The most dramatic event occurred on 27 August during the battle of Bergendal Farm or Dalmanutha. Here, south of Belfast, on the southernmost tip of their line, was the Boers' strongest position, held by about 75 staunch members of the Johannesburg South African Republic Police (ZARPs). After hours of bombardment by 38 guns, the Royal Inniskilling Fusiliers and 2nd Rifle Brigade made a final frontal assault on this boulder-strewn fortress. The ZARPs refused to surrender and few survived this heroic stand which cost the British 120 casualties. During the next four weeks, the Boers retreated steadily east through wild country without being seriously menaced by the British who reached the border station of Koomati Poort on 24 September. As Smith-Dorrien remarked, 'Of the fighting there was very little, for there were not enough enemy to go round with our large numbers.'

On 11 September Kruger, a broken man, left the country, never to return. He sailed from Lourenço Marques for Holland on 19 October. Steyn, meanwhile, had slipped away to rejoin de Wet in the Orange Free State. As they approached the border, the Boers destroyed large quantities of stores and about 2,000 men took refuge in Portuguese East Africa. Thus, once again more of the weaker elements were eliminated, but Botha, Ben Viljoen and other Boer leaders had already escaped in small groups with more than 4,000 men into the remote country either side of the railway. Reitz, who doubled back to continue the struggle, described his adventures: 'We shot a koodoo in the mountain, and made biltong, and we collected a supply of mealies from a neighbouring field. This was all the commissariat we had. The region we traversed (north of the Delagoa Bay railway) was untracked save for native tribes and wild animals.' At

Warm Bath, they found Beyers with a thousand men and remained unmolested for a month. 'We hunted a good deal and several times rode out on patrol to Pienaar's River, 25 miles towards Pretoria, to watch the doing of a large English camp there.' The guerrilla forces of East Transvaal would soon be ready to harry the British as effectively as de la Rey and the Orange Free Staters.

Assuming that the war was virtually ended, on 1 September Roberts formally declared Transvaal to be a British Colony. Early in October Buller was notified that he would be returning to England and the Natal Army as such was broken up.

CHAPTER ELEVEN

The Guerrilla War Explodes

'Fortune takes little or no notice of the shortcomings of the lawyer, of the parson, or the man of business; but the Subaltern who rides into an ambush is criticised and derided at every breakfast-table and his recklessness or misfortune furnishes seeming common sense with a new and unanswered argument against the inefficiency of the whole body of his brother officers.'

Colonel G. F. R. Henderson on the Boer War
(Science of War, *p. 409*).

'He's shoved 'is rifle 'neath my nose
Before I'd time to think,
An' borrowed all my Sunday clo'es.'

Kipling, Piet (*a nickname for the Boer*).

Although a hardened military trouble-shooter, Kitchener was faced with a daunting situation when Roberts left in December, 1900. A full-scale guerrilla war was raging, with endless attacks on the railways, with convoys ambushed, with isolated towns retaken, with Boer commandos openly recruiting in country districts, with great tracts of territory where the British had no control, and with parts of northern Transvaal, including Pietersburg, where British troops had not even penetrated. Thus the classic pattern of a guerrilla conflict prevailed, with the British holding the few major towns and having a tenuous control over the railways by day, while the Boers roamed almost at will through the vast rural areas of Orange Free State and Transvaal. Late in October, 1900, an officer wrote, 'Bloemfontein is practically in a state of siege. The Boers have held up the mail train, and, I presume, collared and destroyed our letters. They have been playing about all round us for two months in parties and small commandos, all well mounted and equipped. They pass their time sniping us, cutting the railway and telegraph lines, shooting at sentries, capturing small detached posts and unprotected convoys. I have just returned with my company from a detached post a few miles north of our camp . . . We stood to arms most nights, and tried to sleep during the day. But the heat in these bell tents is unbearable, and the dust storms too awful to describe, and no shelter anywhere from either. I was alone, and to add to the discomfort we were only allowed one pint of water per man per diem.'

To make matters worse, Kitchener was losing some of his best troops. Many of the Yeomanry and colonial mounted formations had reached the end of their year's contract and were entitled to return home. Roberts' over-optimistic views had led to the ending of recruitment for the Yeomanry and the cessation of horse purchasing from abroad. Admittedly Kitchener had over 200,000 men, but a large proportion were discovered in base camps or other safe administrative jobs and were rooted out, back to active service. The Boers still numbered about 60,000, although there were rarely more than 15,000 in the field. The Boers main advantages were first their mobility—most had at least one pony—and secondly the ease with which they could resume their farming when not needed for operations.

Kitchener was determined to improve the situation. Recruiting was resumed at home and in the colonies, especially the Cape, while many small isolated garrisons were withdrawn. Nevertheless two outstanding administrative problems faced Kitchener. The first was the immediate protection of the railways (the elaborate blockhouse system was yet to be devised), which remained a source of weakness and anxiety. Secondly there was the more intractable problem of good horsemastership. Unless great improvements could be made in the quality of their mounted troops, who were essential in large numbers for defeating the guerrillas, the British would always be at a serious disadvantage against their adversaries to whom the intelligent and economic employment of horses was second nature. The proper training of the mounted troops and supplying them with fit horses plagued the British to the end. Kitchener never seemed able to apply himself consistently and forcefully enough to overcome this complex and unaccustomed problem, which was not amenable to an 'engineer' type of treatment. Fuller's judgement was that 'of the mounted troops we employed the regular cavalry were the least useful, probably because of their fantastic Crusader training. Sticking men with lances and hacking them out of their saddles with swords . . . these otherwise admirable soldiers looked upon a horse not as an aid to mobility but as an article of transportation, lumbering it up with God knows what.' The cavalry expected their horses to carry nearly 300 lbs, whereas the Boers, and Fuller himself, regarded 200 lbs as the normal maximum all-up load. As a result, the cavalry horses were usually easily outpaced by the Boers and the British wastage of animals from exhaustion was very high. The Yeomanry were of uneven quality, many of their officers tending to be foolhardy. Allenby wrote caustically, 'These Yeomanry are useless. After some months in the field, they learn a bit, but by the time they are any use, they have probably been captured two or three times, presenting the Boers on each occasion, with a horse, a rifle and 150 rounds of ammunition.' One gains the impression that experienced British mounted infantry units were good; yet Fuller preferred 'mounted infantry not recruited from the ranks of our Regulars, but from those of the Australians, Canadians, New Zealanders and South Africans, men whose horse sense had not been obliterated by what we are pleased to call "discipline"'. Understandably the Boers feared and disliked the colonials more than the British. By May, 1901, these

horsed troops amounted to 5,000 Australians and New Zealanders, 24,000 South Africans, while a considerable proportion of the newly formed 7,500 South African Constabulary
were also colonials. The rest of the 79,000 mounted troops
consisted of 12,000 Mounted Infantry, 14,000 cavalry and
17,000 Yeomanry. Another shortcoming of the cavalry, in
particular, was their lack of flexibility. Unlike the Boers, they
had a traditional aversion to fighting dismounted, but, except
at very short ranges, were usually incapable of hitting the
enemy with a rifle when mounted, an art in which the Boers
specialized.

As important as the men were the horses. The avoidable
wastage here was prodigious and, besides incompetent
horse-management, was largely attributable to two causes.
First, the remount system was never efficiently organized.
Arriving after a long sea voyage, horses were often immediately sent 1,000 miles or more by rail without being
adequately cared for, and then, so pressing was the demand
for them that they were distributed before either being
acclimatized or fit for active service conditions. Joining the
7th Mounted Infantry in May, 1900, Sgt Jackson recorded
his experiences: 'A Mounted man at last. We had about
three days of extemporised riding school (I could ride quite
well) and then went on duty . . . I got a ripping little black
horse . . . a Bengal Lancer, and I kept him about ten months,
which is a good record for the trekking we did: three months
generally killed them.' His next mount was 'a big Argentine
which had broken down once and had been trekking with the
wagons for a rest, and about the third day's trek we were
away in front going like blazes . . . when he broke down again
and stood with his legs apart and not a move in him . . . I was
left alone on the veld. I ought to have shot him to prevent the
Boers getting him, but let him off.' Next day he visited some
prisoners and took a small pony that he soon swapped for
another Argentine, they were classed as the worst horses,
being large, stupid and vicious. He continues, 'The Old
Argentine was no use at all and I got leave to get a proper

remount which was the second horse I had (you couldn't call the two Argentines remounts, they were both done up before I got them)'. He was lucky to obtain 'a thick-set cobby little mare . . . she looked very fit', probably an Australian horse. Jackson relates how the veterans organized an unofficial remount system from new formations: 'Men from the column with bad horses took them over to the yeomanry lines, and while one engaged the sentry on horse-lines in conversation the other went and took a good horse off the line, putting his own old crock in its place'. To conclude Jackson's story, when a train-load of Hungarian remounts appeared he picked the best, but this was expropriated by the company commander and 'I got a heavy-footed, lumbering old beast with a head like a coal-scuttle and a canter that would fracture your skull!' But there was 'a great raking black mare' which ran away with a young soldier twice in one morning; this was transferred to Jackson, who got his fourth official remount which lasted him till the peace.

The second important reason for the enormous losses of horses was the remorseless way the columns were treated, and this was partly a reflection on Kitchener's methods. Allenby was outspoken about the behaviour of many generals: 'They don't care a straw about the horses . . . I've lost 32 horses in 9 days, only two in action. The rest have died from exhaustion or shortage of food.' On the basis of an average of 50,000 mounted troops each using a minimum of four horses, and remembering that the Artillery and other arms needed tens of thousands of horses, a total of 500,000 horses (350,000 imported) used by the British is easily reached. With most men having two ponies, the Boers must have employed about 200,000 horses. Thus in two and a half years perhaps 750,000 horses were engaged and probably 500,000 of them perished. (The number of horses in Britain today is about 125,000.)

Contemporaries also remarked on the losses of oxen and mules. One officer said that the 75-mile route from Paardeberg to Bloemfontein was marked by dead animal bones; during a fortnight French's cavalry division marched across eastern Transvaal and lost 1,230/2,480 of their oxen. Jackson describes the wasteful ways in which convoys were often organized; he was given charge of 30 loafers from Bloemfontein and 'they took us to the mule lines and told each man to grab two mules. Then each man was given a rickety old Cape Cart'. These were loaded up with oats and, 'It was about a three days' march and I had mules dying every five miles. If there was another mule or horse in sight I stole it, if not, I distributed the load amongst the other carts and burnt the cart'. In contrast, Reitz wrote over a year after the war had started, 'My gentle loyal old roan was as flourishing as ever and I had a fine little chestnut pony, which I had chosen in preference to the larger but less reliable chargers in the English camp.' (Experts regarded English horses as being too big and needing too much feeding.)

To resume the war narrative; on taking over command at the end of November, Kitchener was faced with an emergency in the Orange Free State. The second de Wet hunt was in full cry, but its ramifications stretched back earlier. On 6 November a Mounted Infantry force under Colonel Le Gallais surprised and surrounded de Wet and Steyn at their laager near Bothaville, in north-east Orange Free State. The two Boer leaders only just escaped, leaving some of their followers to fight it out. As one of the most successful British engagements in the guerrilla war, it created a great impression which was accentuated by the gallant death of Le Gallais during the battle. De Wet gave a brief, but characteristic account of this fight: 'Many of the burghers still lay asleep rolled up on their blankets . . . a few of the burghers were making some sort of a stand against the enemy. But all who had already up-saddled were riding away at break-neck speed . . . As I up-saddled my horse I called out to them—"Don't run away. Come back and storm the enemy's position". A panic had seized them . . . The only thing that I could do was to leap into the saddle and try to persuade the fugitives to return. But I did not succeed.' Of the Bothaville battle Jackson reported, 'Each Joe [Boer] as he got his horse or inspanned a Cape cart (which de Wet and Steyn used), cleared on his own to a line of scrub about three-quarters of a mile away, where presumably de Wet (who was the first to clear as usual) re-formed them.' With six guns, nearly 200 Boers were trapped in the farm and its buildings, while another 800 escaped, but some tried to return to help their comrades who were resisting 1,200 British supported by three guns. After five hours, reinforcements arrived and Jackson continued, 'At last some one of the Malta Mounted Infantry shouted "Fix bayonets" . . . just four men *could* fix bayonets, as the majority had been used for picqueting pegs so often that the socket was knocked flat! But the Boers did not know this, and stood up in a body waving anything white . . . Unlike a good many well-known fights, Bothaville *looked* like a battle-field, dead horses everywhere.' Twenty-five Boers were killed, 100 captured and six guns taken, whilst the British lost 13 dead and 33 wounded. 'Nice' Knox (Major-General C.E.) speedily pursued de Wet's force, but they eluded capture by dispersing into small parties.

Despite this reverse, de Wet sprang rapidly back into action. On 11 November he moved southwards, crossing and wrecking the main railway *en route*. By 13 November he gathered 1,500 men and one gun and, on 15 November, easily passed through the line of small British forts that had been constructed eastwards from Bloemfontein to Ladybrand on the Basutoland border. On 23 November he besieged Dewetsdorp (named after his father) where a small garrison was dispersed in poorly-sited shallow trenches; its 480 troops surrendered after two days. Although five other British garrisons were under 50 miles away, only the most distant, and the weakest, made any effort to come to Dewetsdorp, but arrived too late.

It was soon evident that de Wet intended to invade Cape Colony. The new loyalist government there passed stricter measures against rebels, creating discontent amongst the Cape Boers, who were heartened by the failure of the British to pacify the Orange Free State and the Transvaal; thus Cape Colony seemed, to contemporaries, ripe for rebellion. Kitchener acted decisively. The line of the Orange River was considerably reinforced, and most crossings guarded, while Knox was given a strong force of mounted troops. Early in December de Wet crossed the Caledon River heading for the Orange River between Bethulie and Aliwal North, but the weather intervened. Heavy rains made the Caledon and Orange rivers impassable, and it looked as if he was cornered, but just as suddenly the level dropped and, on 7 December, de Wet nipped back across the Caledon. Shedding animals and equipment, he headed north for Smithfield. By forced marches, and making a wide detour, he returned to Dewetsdorp on 12 December and pressed on northwards; the whole time he was attracting more burghers, swelling his force to 4,000.

From 5 December Knox was close on de Wet's tail, once almost catching his rearguard. All British hopes were now pinned on holding de Wet against the chain of hills running from Thabanchu to Ladybrand which lay across his path, and reinforcements were set to block the passes and roads, while Knox came up from behind. Again the line of fortified posts was too thinly held and, on 14 December, after a night march of 30 miles, de Wet detached 500 men to make a feint attack. This deceived the British long enough for the bulk of his force to charge through a 2,000-yard gap held by only 60 of Thorneycroft's men on one side and 100 on the other. An early morning mist making the heliograph inoperative, messages reached other British forces too late. Knox had soon to call off the pursuit, the Boers dispersing into small groups in north-east Orange Free State.

Thus for the second time de Wet escaped, although Kitchener had strained every nerve to trap him. His escape can be attributable partly to good fortune with the weather and the slowness of the British to react, but his outstanding ability was to twist and turn and double back, throwing his pursuers off the scent for a crucial few hours. This was combined with almost inexhaustable energy which he transmitted to his men, and even to his prisoners. Over 400 of these, captured at Dewetsdorp, accompanied de Wet till 5 December and an officer told of marching for 27 hours, the longest halt being one hour. Finally, the Boers had organized their transport system expertly. The same prisoner wrote, 'Boers as a rule, only half-load their wagons; and the great part of their transport consisted of Cape carts, of which they had hundreds. Again the burghers do all their own driving; they have two native boys attached to each wagon, but these do not do the driving, and are only used at the halt to look after the mules and inspan and outspan when there is no immediate hurry . . . during the trek they had only two ox wagons.' The British lacked this vigorousness, yet in fairness it must be emphasized that many of their mounted troops had, between March and November, covered 4,000 miles on the veld, and few had had more than a fortnight's rest.

Although de Wet's prestige was further enhanced, this invasion foray was largely unproductive, except that, in the excitement of the de Wet hunt, Hertzog with nearly 1,200 and Kritzinger with 700 men were, on 16 December, able to slip into Cape Colony. As *The Times* reported on 2 January, 1901, 'The immediate aspect of affairs in Cape Colony . . . is scarcely less gloomy than at the beginning of 1900.' With hindsight, these incursions can be regarded as almost devoid of military significance, but at the time the facility with which these hostile bands operated created an atmosphere of consternation. Having almost no transport and aided by most of the local populace, the guerrillas easily evaded pursuing columns. They damaged railways, destroyed communications and ambushed small bodies of troops. Hertzog moved steadily west, some of his followers gaining the coast at Lambert's Bay, 150 miles north of Cape Town, where they expected to find a foreign vessel loaded with arms, but instead were greeted by some shots from a waiting British cruiser! Kritzinger's force turned southwards and penetrated almost to the coast near Port Elizabeth; he was pursued by Haig, French's chief staff officer, whom Kitchener singled out for this strenuous task. Martial law was proclaimed over a considerable area of Cape Colony, and local loyalists were hurriedly recruited to guard towns and railways. Yet, with all this display of vigour and daring, Hertzog and Kritzinger could neither recruit many new supporters, nor induce a mass rising among the Boers and by mid-February they retraced their steps towards the Orange River.

By the end of January, 1901, South Africa was in ferment. The situation therefore seemed propitious for carrying out a grandiose scheme concocted earlier by Steyn and the Transvaalers for a simultaneous invasion of Natal by Botha and Cape Colony by de Wet. His previous attempt had primarily been a diversion, to assist Botha to recruit volunteers. He also expected Hertzog and Kritzinger to ferment risings, before he joined forces with them on his return to Cape Colony. Kitchener was preparing counter-measures to smash Botha, but these had to be postponed.

Such was the resilience of the Free State guerrillas that, a mere five weeks after their first rebuff, de Wet was able to assemble 2,200 men. On 27 January, accompanied by Steyn, he marched south from near Senekal. Forewarned, Kitchener tried to bar his route, but de Wet eluded the columns under Knox and Bruce Hamilton. Kitchener next planned to hold de Wet on the Orange River, and he hurriedly collected mounted troops, dispatching them southwards by rail. He brought Lyttelton from Transvaal to take charge of operations. Lyttelton did not know the region, whereas French did and would have been a better choice. Proving the ineffectiveness of trying to hold a river line, de Wet misled the British, crossing the Orange River on 10 February, but 800 of his Free Staters refused to accompany him. Moving westwards, he was at first assisted by terrible weather which flooded the river, marooning powerful British columns on the northern bank. De Wet hoped to join Hertzog, but they failed to synchronize their movements. From 12 to 19 February he was closely pursued by Plumer, perhaps the most forceful of the British column commanders, the majority of whose troops were Australians. De Wet's predicament was now worsened by the torrential rain and he abandoned most of his transport, but on 15 February he crossed the railway about 30 miles north of de Aar. The next day Kitchener arrived there to arrange a systematic plan of action. His object was to keep de Wet from breaking south and entering the more populated districts of Cape Colony. Kitchener organized fifteen columns, totalling 15,000 men, who could successively take up the chase, using the railways to give them the maximum mobility. Kitchener also wanted to prevent any junction between de Wet and Hertzog who was entering the area.

Although outmanoeuvred, de Wet's capture was not imminent. On 19 February, he forsook the idea of invading Cape Colony and sought to return to the Free State, but was hemmed in by the flooded Orange River, and by the railways. From 21 to 28 February he doubled back eastwards, following the Orange upstream for nearly 200 miles and tried fourteen different fords, finding them all impassable. His position seemed desperate, especially after 24 February, when he recrossed the railway south of the Orange River Station; he was then cornered in a quadrilateral with railways on three sides and the Orange River on the north. Owing to poor communications, congestion on the railways, and bad scouting on the British part, and by clever rearguard actions and prodigious marches, often at night, de Wet always just managed to slip through the cordons or out-distance the nearest column till it wearied. On 27 February Hertzog linked up with de Wet and, on the 28th, they crossed at the obscure Botha's Drift, virtually unopposed. Guarding this stretch of the Orange, Byng was helpless, having only 200 men to cover 25 miles of front. De Wet wrote, 'I can hardly describe the different exclamations of joy, the Psalms and the songs that now rose up from the burghers splashing through the water. "Never will we return", "No more of the Colony

for me", "On to the Free State".' De Wet and the Free
Staters never did return. Although Plumer and others
continued the chase, it was a hopeless task, de Wet's men
melting away as he fled north. By 2 March he was back near
Senekal, having covered over 800 miles in 43 days, and
escaped the clutches of over 15,000 troops. The third de Wet
hunt further enhanced his prestige and, once in his native
land, the British had little prospect of capturing him, but
until they could do so, there was no likelihood of the Free
Staters giving up their struggle. On the other hand, his two
attempted invasions had shown that, although feeling dis-
contented, and eager to succour rebels, the Cape Boers
recoiled from being led into a general rising.

With de Wet stealing the limelight and some of their
troops being removed to pursue him, British commanders in
western Transvaal, where there was little or no fighting,
tended to become too complacent and sent convoys out with
inadequate escorts. Early in December, de la Rey began an
offensive by capturing 138 wagons and over 1,800 oxen and
inflicting over 100 casualties. Soon afterwards, he and
Beyers joined forces, with over 3,000 men. Although they had
been near him for some days, this information was not passed
on to General Clements who had stopped with a large convoy
at Noitgedacht in the Megaliesberg, 40 miles west of
Pretoria. The unsuspecting Clements' camp was ill-sited, being
directly beneath a precipitous cliff from which Reitz recalled,
'I could look straight down into the English camp hundreds
of feet below. I could almost have dropped a pebble upon the
running soldiers and the white-tented streets and long lines
of picketed horses'. On 13 December Beyers, with 1,500 men,
overwhelmed the defenders on the heights above, while de la
Rey simultaneously attacked those guarding the camp itself.
Clements extricated about 1,000 of the troops, but lost 640,
including 74 killed; he would have suffered even more
severely if the loot had not been so attractive. French was
quickly dispatched to restore order in the Magaliesberg, and
temporarily broke up de la Rey's group. Beyers moved off

eastwards, blew up the railway a dozen miles north of Johannesburg, and then turned northwards to get safely away with his wagons. At the end of January, having served his apprenticeship with de la Rey, Jan Smuts began his career as a brilliant independent guerrilla leader. He chose the Gatsrand ridge, near Johannesburg, for his operations.

Kitchener was also faced with a renewal of guerrilla actions against the isolated garrisons guarding the Delagoa Bay railway. At the end of December Viljoen surprised and overran the 200 troops in the small post at Helvetia and removed a 4·7 in. gun. Soon afterwards, a more ambitious combined assault on Belfast, by both Viljoen and Botha, was repulsed by Smith-Dorrien's troops who suffered over 170 casualties. Judging the most dangerous threat to be Botha's guerrillas in eastern Transvaal, Kitchener, late in January, launched his first major offensive there. French commanded the operation with 8,500 mounted troops, who were encumbered with over 6,000 infantry and 63 guns, while a further 6,000 men were organized to supply them. Kitchener evolved an enterprising plan to rid over 20,000 square miles both of the guerrilla bands and of their means of sustenance. This offensive was modelled on a huge shoot, the beaters and their guns consisting of seven columns. Starting first were five columns who were to advance parallel in an easterly direction from the Pretoria–Orange Free State railway, with the Delagoa Bay railway on their northern and the Natal railway on their southern flanks. Two other columns (There should have been three, but Paget's column, which included Plumer, had been sent away to chase de Wet.) were to start six days later, from the Delagoa Bay railway and sweep southwards. Thus, in theory, the Boers would either be trapped or forced to fight it out. To succeed, this 'drive' depended on meticulous and constant coordination, on continuous communication and precise timing, otherwise gaps would soon form between both the parallel and the converging columns, permitting the more determined Boers to break back and escape the net, and this was what soon happened. As the columns approached Ermelo, the main town in the district, Botha realized the danger. He concentrated 2,000 men against Smith-Dorrien, whose column was the largest and most isolated. Under cover of thick fog very early on 6 February, Botha's men fell on Smith-Dorrien's camp and almost overran it. 'Horses and, I am ashamed to say, men too were stampeding everywhere . . . but it was the rush of the horses, really most alarming, which created the temporary panic,' Smith-Dorrien wrote. After a brief, fierce skirmish, the Boers were repulsèd, but Botha broke through the cordon, as elsewhere several smaller groups had done earlier and others were to do later.

Pausing near Ermelo to regroup, the somewhat depleted columns then trundled towards the Swaziland and Natal borders. Once they entered this rugged region, the drive was beset with ever-increasing hardships and handicaps. The men and horses suffered from the terrible weather and shortages of all kinds of supplies. By mid-April when the drive was ending, a column commander recorded that 667 of his 1,838 mounted troops were 'on foot and the remainder on enfeebled horses . . . but Lord Kitchener says that he is quite unable to provide any remounts'. Meeting little opposition, the military commanders' efforts became diverted into carrying out the scorched-earth policy. Smith-Dorrien related, 'I had over 20,000 sheep. My orders were not to leave any food for the Boers, but how to drive these flocks and herds along was a puzzle . . . Before we moved on we had to slaughter 15,000 sheep'. When the drive petered out after eleven weeks, the official bag was 272,752 head of stock, 2,281 carts, 11 guns and a mere 1,350 Boers, over half of whom had surrendered voluntarily.

The offensive in eastern Transvaal had two important repercussions. Botha was compelled to cancel his projected invasion of Natal, scheduled to coincide with de Wet's invasion of Cape Colony. Secondly, Kitchener reckoned that the effects of French's drive might persuade Botha to discuss peace proposals. He therefore approached Mrs Botha, then living in Pretoria, to send a letter to her husband. Receiving an encouraging reply, Kitchener went to Middelburg where, on 28 February, he met Botha under a flag of truce. Kitchener always considered Botha would try to end the war if offered relatively moderate terms, and the talks were cordial. Kitchener would not negotiate on the issue of independence, as Botha wanted, but was ready to agree to lenient terms for the Cape and Natal rebels. A draft of the proposals was sent to both Milner and the home government, which modified most of the terms adversely for the Boers, refused to grant an amnesty to the 300 or so leading rebels, rendering them liable to be court-martialled and shot. Kitchener wrote angrily to Broderick, 'My views are that once the Boers gave up their independence and laid down their arms, the main object of government was attained.' Botha, also acting unilaterally, was not yet convinced the war was irretrievably lost, and, as was subsequently proved, it was most improbable that he could then have swayed Smuts, let alone Steyn and de Wet and other hard-line local leaders. Botha rejected the terms and the war dragged on. (A minor but pleasant outcome to the Middelburg Conference was that Kitchener introduced Botha to bridge, a game to which he immediately became an addict; on parting Kitchener presented the Boers with 50 packs of cards.)

Before the winter limited operations Kitchener sent columns into the extensive, but sparsely inhabited, region of Transvaal north of the Delagoa Bay railway. Almost unopposed, Plumer marched 200 miles from Pretoria up the railway to Pietersburg, reaching there on 8 April. The temporary capital of Transvaal, this town had never been occupied by the British and was the centre of a prosperous farming area which supported Beyers' commandos. During the subsequent phase of operations, Plumer turned southwards towards the Delagoa Bay railway from whence six columns splayed out, advancing northwards towards him, the whole force of 11,000 being under General Sir Bindon Blood's command. Besides a scorched-earth policy, the columns aimed at converging to catch the Transvaal government of Schalk Burger, ensconsed in the hills north of Belfast, but the more important prize was Ben Viljoen's 1,100 men. Except for blowing up the railway, usually done by Captain Hindon who specialized in this form of sabotage, Viljoen's men had been inactive for some months. Both Schalk Burger and Viljoen evaded the British by crossing the railway towards Ermelo, but over 100 of Viljoen's men surrendered during the chase. After destroying some farms, flour mills and crops, which had a negligible effect in this fertile district, the drive ended early in May with almost all the 1,100 Boers having surrendered voluntarily.

Finally, why Kitchener regarded a Boer collapse in eastern Transvaal as a reasonable possibility can be appreciated from this letter written by Smith-Dorrien from Belfast on 22 January: 'I have had some most interesting communications with Generals Louis Botha and Ben Viljoen lately under a flag of truce . . . Their tone is much more civil since their attack on this place was repulsed. Ben Viljoen used to be very rough to our prisoners, but now he is quite the contrary. He sent in one day to say if there were any letters for the prisoners . . . I sent them out with a letter of thanks and asked if I could send him anything . . . He asked for some claret, and I sent him two cases a day or two later. He sent me a Kruger sovereign, which he wished me to keep as a keepsake and to have engraved "General Ben Viljoen to General S-D".' (He had it made into a bracelet for his mother.) Even in the eighteenth century war rarely reached these heights of amiability!

CHAPTER TWELVE

Blockhouses and Drives

'I wish those who say that the war should be over would come out and show us how to do it.'

Kitchener, in a letter to Roberts, 1902.

'When the choice seemed to be between capture or annihilation, I came to count, as a fixed factor, on the nervous shyness of the enemy, on an aversion to the last embrace with the Boers.'

From Smuts, on the reason for the British failure to crush the commandos.

May, 1901, is a useful date to pause and take stock of the situation. During the next and final year, the character of the war altered slowly but appreciably. Kitchener rapidly extended the chains of blockhouses, which reduced the Boers' freedom of movement and this, combined with the scorched-earth policy, increasingly restricted their ability to wage guerrilla war. The British drives became more frequent and systematized and these, despite many shortcomings, so harried the Boers that numbers of them lost heart and surrendered. Being a period composed chiefly of skirmishing, it would be wearisome to follow the war in detail, instead some contemporary accounts will be selected to describe how it was fought.

Although the Irish Brigade had now been disbanded, Blake survived uncaptured till the end of the war. His descriptions of the last phase of the war in eastern Transvaal are revealing: 'The Boers were divided up into small bands 100, 200 or 300 strong, and each little band went as it pleased, and when it pleased, but generally confined itself to its own little district. These small commands were always in close touch with each other and could quickly come together if there was a chance of taking in some single English column that might be passing by. During the day, when not fighting, we would camp near some old ruins where we would find a little patch of grass that had escaped the fire. The English would generally see us and we were sure to see them at all times. After sunset and darkness had set in, we would saddle up, dodge behind the English, find another little patch of grass, and then unsaddle, hobble our horses and try to get a little sleep. So cold it was that precious little any of us had during the night. We would put out no guards, but at four o'clock in the morning all would get their horses, saddle up and prepare to fight. We would then send out a man here and there, say about 1,000 yards distance, to wait for daylight and to locate the English if possible. If none were to be seen at hand after the sun came up, we would unsaddle, hobble our horses again and try to get in some sleep under the warm sunshine. If the English were found near, we would probably have a short skirmish with them, knock a few from their horses, and then fly away to some other part of our district.'

The Boers were ingenious in feeding themselves and Blake continues: 'Before the rainy season set in, about October, the burghers would pull out their hidden plows, put the fields in good shape and then plant their mealies (maize). All this had to be done under the cover of darkness . . . In the following March and April we would have plenty of green mealies, and, later on, dry mealies. The English could not destroy these crops, though they tried and failed. If they turned their horses out to eat and trample it down, the green corn would kill them. When the corn ripened and became dry they tried to burn it, but failed because there was little or no grass in the fields. The result was that we had mealies on the stalk in all districts. Many would be gathered, hidden in the high reeds along the small rivers, or buried in nice, dry pits. The English have often ridden over these without discovering them . . . We always had cattle nearby and generally two or three good fat bullocks with us . . . The English would capture our cattle today and make their report. Tomorrow, we would take the cattle back, but the English would make no report.' In season, the Boers ate fresh fruit and vegetables. They carried little hand coffee mills with them to turn maize into a coarse sort of meal. Fuel was invariably short, but they used cow dung. Blake described the Boer diet: 'for breakfast, a small tin pot filled with water would be brought to the boiling point, the meal carefully stirred in and constantly stirred for about forty minutes, when it would be cooked. Of course we had no salt; so our fresh meat would be thrown into the ashes, broiled to suit each one's taste . . . There is ammonia or some kind of salts in the ashes, that help the meat out. For coffee . . . some meal would be burnt in a small pan, till black, and then put into the boiling water; . . . We lived this way for two long years, fighting all the time or trying to evade the English, and we lost but one man from sickness.'

By this time, nearly all the Mauser ammunition had been expended, but most Boers had re-equipped themselves with British rifles. As Reitz emphasized, ammunition was for these weapons no problem: 'During the next two days we followed the road by which the English force had travelled, to pick up Lee-Metford cartridges . . . it had become a regular practice to trail the columns.' It is difficult to estimate the number of combatant Boers, but out of 44,000 men of all ages at large in May, 1901, it was thought that less than 15,000 were in the field at any one time. Between May, 1901, and May, 1902, the Boer losses were reckoned at about 25,000, of whom 19,500 either surrendered or were captured, 2,000 being killed and the remainder wounded. Of the 20,000 still on some form of active service in May, 1902, 3,500 were classified as rebels, renegades or foreigners.

For the British, statistics are hard to interpret accurately, but probably their battle casualties were much the same as the Boers, although disease, especially typhoid, took a heavier toll. Theoretically, in May, 1901, Kitchener had 240,000 men, but this is a distorted figure. Breaking down this total, about 25,000 were South Africans and mostly confined to local guard duties in Cape Colony; 105,000 were in the infantry and militia; 17,000 were artillerymen and engineers; 11,500 were in the Army Service or Medical Corps, and finally about 80,000 were mounted troops, of whom nearly 30,000 were colonials. Yet an official return of the fighting strength for 19 June, 1901, listed only 164,000 men, but this excluded the sick, the locally employed Cape troops and 7,500 South African Constabulary. To complicate the picture further, by May, 1902, thousands of non-white scouts had been armed for blockhouse guard duties and for gathering information. If caught, no mercy was shown to these men. Jackson wrote, 'There was a Colonial doing intelligence officer. He used to go out with six or eight Kaffirs and scout about. One day he didn't come back so next day they sent the ambulance out and found his six boys shot and laid out by the side of the road. He turned up a fortnight after.' It was not an entirely one-sided business. Jackson also recalled how another patrol went out, without a white officer, and, 'four or five Boers, not seeing till too late that they were Kaffirs came down to surrender. The Kaffirs took their rifles and then shot the lot!'

During the latter part of the war, service for most British troops became a matter of extremes. Either they led highly active lives, pursuing the enemy in the field, or they endured a static existence, as did the majority of infantry who were locked up in blockhouses. These were originally built to protect the railways, but after June, 1901, were extended to protect roads between towns in the more affected areas, and to guard some river lines. Eventually chains of blockhouses (over 8,000 were built) covered about 3,700 miles. Designed by Major Rice, a blockhouse could be assembled in only six hours by six trained engineers and a few infantrymen. It consisted of two circular skins of corrugated iron six inches apart, the gap between being filled with rubble, and the whole structure was surmounted by a gabled roof. The interior diameter was 13 feet, and the headroom about 6 feet. The entrance was by a small door shielded by a bullet-proof metal sheet and in the walls were 12 rifle slits. The lower part of the structure was strengthened by a wall of stones and earth, and every blockhouse had its water tanks, reserves of food and ammunition and a telephone. Encircling each one was a deep perimeter trench and a high wire fence. Linking it with the two neighbouring blockhouses were thick wire fences hung with tin cans as alarm warnings. These wire entanglements were sited at such an angle that those firing along them would not hit the next door blockhouses about 1,000 yards away. At night, armed native scouts patrolled the intervening areas, and armoured trains were on call. A blockhouse was normally manned by a corporal and six men. A subaltern would command three or four blockhouses, a captain ten or twelve, while a battalion might have upwards of 60 under its command. Fuller wrote of their demoralizing influence: 'Apart from sentry duty and minor fatigue work there was absolutely nothing to do except talk, smoke and gamble. Frequently no sign of civilization, or even of life, except from the two neighbouring blockhouses, could be seen for miles around . . . almost unceasing sentry go, lack of natural exercise and monotony of food told on the nerves. Though they were in complete safety men would become jumpy and bad tempered . . . Directly one blockhouse fired, the chances were that a veritable *feu de terreur* would run down the line. On one occasion fire was actually carried . . . down a line of some 120 blockhouses.'

In addition to restricting the Boers' freedom of movement, blockhouse lines provided the British with relatively firm flanks during their drives, and with secure routes along which to send supplies to outlying formations. The blockhouses were, however, never expected to form impregnable barriers. Reitz's experiences of their obstructiveness was fairly typical; in July, 1901, with a handful of men, he failed to cross the railway south of Bloemfontein, but in August, at the same place, 30 of them broke through because 'we were with men who knew the exact position of every blockhouse and every sentry along the track and by midnight we were over without a single casualty, although there was a good deal of firing'. During 1901–1902 these kind of huge spiders' webs steadily enmeshed the country where the guerrillas operated and even experts, like de Wet, found it increasingly difficult and costly to break through them. Yet the standards of alertness, determination and marksmanship of those manning them were sometimes deplorable. Between 6–15 March, 1902, accompanied by Steyn and 200 men, de Wet crossed unscathed three blockhouse lines, first between Heilbron and Frankfort, then on the main railway just south of Vereeniging and finally at the Valsch River, to enter Transvaal.

To turn to the employment of the mobile troops. As their numbers grew and they became more experienced, Kitchener devised for them frequent and ever more elaborately organized drives. These were concentrated against three most affected areas, north-eastern Free State, eastern Transvaal, and north-western Transvaal. The drive against de Wet, starting on 6 February, exemplified the minute detail with which Kitchener planned these operations. Between the 54 miles separating Frankfort in the north and Kaffir Kop in the south were placed the four columns of Rawlinson, Byng, Rimington and Elliot. Their 9,000 men were spaced out at an average of one man per ten yards. With their flanks resting on blockhouse lines, they were to advance 50 miles westwards to drive their prey against the barrier of the Central Railway. This whole operation was to last only three days. By day, the column commanders had a fairly free hand in the methods they adopted for advancing the prescribed distance, but for the night, Kitchener issued the following detailed instructions:

'1. Every man from Brigadier to the last native to be on duty and to act as sentry for one-third of the night.
2. Front Line—Each squadron to be allotted a length of front, to be covered by intrenched pickets of six men, 50

21 and 22 Two views of troops on active service taken from *A Soldier's Diary* by Murray Cosby Jackson, who fought in South Africa from 1899 to 1901. (*Above*) the Burmah Mounted Infantry—these soldiers were volunteers who brought their own ponies from Burma. (*Below*) a young Imperial Yeomanry soldier, the answer to a Boer's prayer!

23 The Kaap River Bridge near Koomati Poort. This illustration shows the bridge damaged by the Boers, a deviation bridge and the wreck of a train.

24 A blockhouse under construction surrounded by its protecting wire fence.

to 100 yards apart . . . Guns loaded with case to be posted in front line, officers and men to form similar posts of six, strengthened by small infantry escorts. Transports, artillery vehicles and all horses to be in small laagers, handy to their units.

3. Rear Line—A thin rear line of pickets each of six men, 500 yards in rear of front line; two pickets to a mile. If attacked, to fall back on the laagers.

4. Sham Front Line—A sham line of pickets to be taken up by daylight, a mile or two in front of the real line, and evacuated after dark, fires to be left burning along it. Two real lines to be selected by daylight, but on no account to be occupied till after dark.'

Despite these precautions, de Wet soon broke through the blockhouse line on the southern flank, while other groups also slipped through the net elsewhere. Of an estimated 1,800 Boers in this area, the bag was only 286. Within a few days, other smaller drives were begun. At the end of February, a second major drive was started. Counting those in static positions, 30,000 troops were employed (de Wet claimed 60,000). This drive nearly succeeded. The main prizes, de Wet and Steyn, were almost cornered and lost 50 killed and 778 captured. Their casualties included a boy of 13; of these youths, Jackson said, 'lots of released prisoners say they owed their release to the old chaps, for the youngsters of 14 and 15 wanted to shoot them.' Kitchener harried this part of Orange Free State with another large drive early in March, but the 'bag' was very small, de Wet and Steyn escaping again. Yet this continued harassment and the fact their two leaders soon afterwards quit the country, seriously depressed Boer morale in this region.

On the other side of the Vaal, Boer hopes were suddenly revived by de la Rey's activities. After months of relative inaction, he gained two quick successes. Late in February, he seized a convoy near Klerksdorp (at Yzer Spruit) inflicting 500 casualties, including 300 prisoners. Although the

6

convoy's guard put up a stout resistance and their artillery
fire could be heard by formations in the vicinity, no help was
sent till too late. De la Rey's second victory was far more
sensational, but equally well deserved. On 2 March Methuen
set out eastwards from Vryburg with a convoy of 39 oxen and
46 mule wagons, escorted by 1,400 troops of very mixed
quality, including mounted irregulars. After five days' march
through largely waterless country where the British had no
troops, Methuen intended to join Colonel Grenfell's column
of 1,500 mounted men who were starting from Klerksdorp;
but the arrangements for their juncture were very vague.
Once united, Methuen hoped to search out and defeat the
Boer leader, whom he had been fighting for over two years.
De la Rey watched Methuen's approach and, on 7 March,
struck with 1,500 men at Tweebosch. The irregular troops
soon fled, the remainder resisting bravely for some hours
before being overwhelmed. The British lost nearly 800 with
68 killed and 121 wounded, including Methuen. With
characteristic chivalry, de la Rey saw that the badly wounded
General received medical care, and dispatched a messenger to
let his wife know of her husband's plight! When the news of
this disaster was broken to Kitchener, he wept and, for nearly
two days, shut himself up alone.

To turn now to events in eastern Transvaal, early in
September, 1901, Botha eventually set forth on his cherished
project of invading Natal. Militarily this was a very different
proposition from invading Cape Colony because the approach
march was longer and more difficult and because the people
of Natal were hostile to the Boer cause. Although the British
had been forewarned, Botha, with 2,000 men, reached,
undetected, the Vryheid region on the Transvaal–Natal
border. On 16 September he overwhelmed a British mounted
column under Gough, capturing most of its 300 soldiers and
killing or wounding nearly all the remainder. Ten days later,
Botha attacked British posts at Mount Itala and at Fort
Prospect, but was repulsed in both places and his offensive
petered out. At the beginning of October, he began what

should have been a perilous return journey through almost trackless territory where the British had sent considerable forces to cut him off. But burdened, in Kitchener's words, with 'kitchen ranges, pianos and harmoniums', the various uncoordinated British columns were soon outpaced by Botha who jettisoned his transport. By mid October, Botha was safely back in eastern Transvaal.

Botha's hasty return was partly because reports were reaching him of widespread disaffection amongst the burghers. They were becoming extremely despondent owing to a series of punitive night raids during August and September when they lost over 200 men. These British successes in the Carolina, Ermelo and Bethal areas, were the result of the combined efforts of two remarkable men. The leader was Colonel Benson, of Magersfontein fame, who had trained a body of mounted troops and artillery to undertake a surprise attack after riding for over 40 miles silently at night. His small column acted on intelligence provided by a prominent Uitlander, Colonel Woolls-Sampson, who had been largely responsible for raising the Imperial Light Horse. Severely wounded early in the Natal campaign, he was later given command of this regiment, but it suffered heavy losses at Cypherfontein in January, 1901, and he was relieved of his command. He then exploited his extensive knowledge of eastern Transvaal by recruiting and training there a small body of native scouts who specialized in gaining, from local natives, up-to-date information on the movements of guerrilla bands. Guided by these scouts, Benson timed his forays meticulously to pounce on the Boer laagers just before dawn. Although Benson never captured a complete group, the Boers lost many soldiers who were often without horses on which to escape. Even more important was the psychological effect of the raids on the burghers' nerves, because between their bouts of military activities the guerrillas relied on periods of rest. These recuperative spells were now being eroded, and, if his men were to remain loyal, Botha knew he must quickly destroy Benson's column.

Botha had three immediate advantages over Benson. First, with the local men and those returning with him from Natal, he could, at short notice, always outnumber his adversary who had 1,400 troops of whom only two-thirds were mounted. Secondly, his invasion of Natal had drawn off almost all the mobile British forces, thus Benson could not be reinforced rapidly. Thirdly Botha was aware that Benson had to protect his travelling supply depot of 120 ox wagons, and it was this encumbrance that Botha skilfully used to bring about Benson's downfall.

When Benson resumed his night raids in October, some of his experienced units had been replaced with untried ones. He now found the Boers more wary and aggressive and he had to fend off frequent probing attacks. On 30 October, some of his wagons became bogged down and he collected a rearguard force to protect them. Informed of Benson's difficulties, Botha made a lightning march of 70 miles with 500 men to reinforce Grobler, the local commander. Splitting his forces, Botha sent a strong detachment to attack Woolls-Sampson in an entrenched camp near Bakenlaagte, 20 miles north of Carolina. The Boers failed to storm the camp, but did prevent any help being sent from the main British body to Benson, less than a mile away. With 1,200 mounted men, Botha drove back Benson's isolated rearguard of 280 men and two guns. The Boers pinned the British down on a little ridge, known as Gun Hill. Here Benson fought to the last and was among the 66 killed. In this most dramatic action, the Boers suffered comparatively heavily, but Botha had brilliantly vindicated his authority. From November onwards eastern Transvaal was placed under Bruce Hamilton. He continued the night raids and several large drives were organized, without achieving significant results. But, together with systematic farm burning, these measures helped to produce a mounting sense of war-weariness among the commandos in a region where the natives were hostile. In February Botha quit the region and returned to the Vryheid district.

North of the Delagoa Bay railway little fighting took

place. Nominally under Ben Viljoen, the Boers' commandos had grown accustomed to a quiet life, which the British rarely disturbed. On 25 January, 1902, after visiting the acting President Burger, Viljoen was captured near Lydenburg by a patrol. Although the most senior guerrilla officer taken prisoner in the war, by then Viljoen's authority had so declined that his capture had little effect on Boer morale.

CHAPTER THIRTEEN

The Final Phase

'I have nothing to do with facts. The entire war is a matter of faith.'

De Wet during the Peace discussions.

'Boer women were bitter and irreconcilable . . . Sometimes a girl might talk a bit but all the time . . . you would be well aware of the meaning of those quick glances at the far horizon and that she was praying all she knew to God Almighty that de la Rey and his bold riders might come galloping over the skyline.'

Ian Hamilton.

The final peace negotiations began on 12 April, 1902. Kitchener having been Commander-in-Chief for nearly eighteen months, this is a convenient time to consider some of his failings and achievements. Kitchener's main virtues were his energy, his thoroughness, his decisiveness and his quickness in grasping detail. Yet these were also a source of weakness, making him into an isolated figure unable easily to delegate authority. Writing to Chamberlain, in October, 1901, Churchill asserted, 'Kitchener is overworked, exhausts himself on many unimportant details and is now showing signs of prolonged strain. There is no plan worth speaking of in the operations except hammer, hammer at random.' Allenby complained of the treatment of subordinate column commanders: 'One is always at high pressure . . . one is probably only under the same general for about a month at a time. When he has played about and knocked one's column to rags, he goes off.' (Between April and November, 1901, Rawlinson's column covered 2,500 miles.)

With the war seemingly dragging on endlessly, Kitchener was subjected to widespread criticism. In particular, the autocratic Milner felt frustrated by Kitchener's domineering behaviour, especially over the concentration camps. Moreover, despite Kitchener sending French there in June, 1901, and giving him a free hand with over 8,000 mobile troops, Cape Colony was still plagued by small guerrilla bands. Admittedly Scheepers and Kritzinger were eventually captured, while Lotter was seized and executed for treason, but Malan and Fouché and others were never caught. Indeed, the situation deteriorated. In September, 1901, Smuts, after an adventurous journey, established himself in the remote north-western Cape Colony, compelling Milner to continue martial law. In desperation, on 1 November Milner wrote to Chamberlain, 'Is it not possible to tell Kitchener that he is wanted in India? . . . not because anyone else will conduct the War better, but because someone else may, if put in on that distinct understanding, obstruct the work of reconstruction less. I should not make the suggestion if we had not got Lyttelton.' Chamberlain was unconvinced and Lord Salisbury demolished this proposal by stating, 'We must know much more fully in detail what it is that Milner has asked in vain of Kitchener before we make it a ground for superseding Kitchener by a Commander chosen by Milner'. (Suspecting that he might be out of favour, Kitchener had earlier offered his resignation, but this was immediately rejected.)

Kitchener inherited Roberts' system of concentration camps, their official British name. (The term was later used by the Nazis for their notorious extermination camps.) The numbers of homeless increased rapidly during the early part of the guerrilla war, and more of these mainly tented camps were hurriedly set up. Water and sanitary facilities were often utterly inadequate and these deficiences were aggravated by the lack of hygiene among the rural Boers, who had rarely had any experience of communal existence. By May, 1901, 36 camps housed nearly 100,000 refugees, about half of whom were children. The extremely high mortality rates were initially caused by the fact that so many were already suffering from exposure when brought in. The health of the inmates was further undermined by shortages of fresh food, especially milk. The lack of resistance to epidemics, such as measles, and the determination of mothers to nurse their sick children without informing the camp staff, contributed to the terrible mortality rate. The callousness and incompetence of some of those originally charged with the administration of camps exacerbated the problems created by the overcrowding, and by the disruption of supplies because of the war. Early in 1901 Miss Hobhouse visited some camps and her lurid revelations led some foreign papers to allege that the British were trying to exterminate the Boer women and children. In the second half of 1901, the Government sent out a Commission of Ladies to inspect the camps, and many of their recommendations were carried out. Already removed from military control, conditions had greatly improved and the death-rate had dropped steeply. Although this scandal did lasting damage to the British cause, it must be stressed that, in principle, the Boers welcomed these camps. Their dependants seriously restricted their mobility and their fighting capacity, because, in many parts, the natives were hostile and it was unsafe to leave unprotected groups of women and children. A prisoner of war wrote of 'a service that the English have done us in taking away our womenfolk. However severely the defenceless victims of the war have had to suffer, they would have had a much worse time of it and made our continuous resistance well-nigh impossible, if the enemy had left them among us' (quoted by Lyttelton). Botha expressed much the same opinion. In December, Kitchener recognized the military value to the Boers of these camps and banned further intakes.

Although with hindsight Kitchener's conduct of the campaign has been criticized on several counts, his achievements were monumental. By April, 1902, the ever-lengthening lines of blockhouses and forts even further contracted the areas within which the Boers could operate securely. The policy of farm-burning was admittedly partly counter-productive, hardening the resolve to continue fighting among many of those who had lost everything. But soldiers could not be expected to spare property which was being openly used for sanctuary by their enemy. Furthermore, the widespread devastation cast a pall of hopelessness, gradually affecting even the bravest spirits.

Only a somewhat inconclusive answer can be returned to the question of whether Kitchener's reforms could have produced an army eventually capable of crushing the guerrillas in the field. When any large force continually receives raw troops who have to be employed almost immediately, the quality of individual units becomes uneven. This factor resulted in some humiliating reverses, as when a detachment of the Lovat Scouts was surprised and badly cut up by Kritzinger in September, 1901. Understandably, with both sides dressed much alike, large slouch hats being generally worn by horsemen, it was often hard, even for experienced campaigners, to distinguish immediately friend from foe. During the beginning of the Roodewall battle of 11 April, 1902, the impression was that Commandant Kemp's men belonged to Rawlinson's column, but, 'Then from the plain in front, a single horseman, galloping furiously up to Grenfell, shouted, "They are Boers; all those men are Boers".' On other occasions, troops over-reacted and fired on their comrades. Sensational minor defeats were sometimes caused by the impetuosity of junior leaders falling for a favourite Boer ruse of sending out a small and apparently isolated patrol. Troops would then pursue the Boers who lured them on to where a force was waiting which outnumbered them, as happened to Gough at Blood River Poort in September, 1901. Suffering the occasional 'bloody nose' is an inevitable feature of guerrilla war, and was less reprehensible than the dilatoriness and over-caution shown by some British commanders, like Kitchener's brother General Walter, who frequently refused to take reasonable risks. (See Kipling's poem, 'Two Kopjes'.)

Kitchener has been criticized for not destroying more of the Boer forces and for failing to capture their major leaders. But as the war continued, the Boer ranks were greatly reduced, until only the most dedicated and combat-hardened fighters remained. They had an inherent advantage over a Regular Army, in that, when pressed, they could always justifiably disencumber themselves of impedimenta, such as guns. As de Wet demonstrated, by not entangling with their opponents, lightly equipped formations can normally escape even the most meticulously prepared encircling movements. Kitchener had the almost insuperable task of trying to eliminate dozens of small guerrilla groups scattered over a largely roadless territory about the extent of France, the Low Countries and East and West Germany combined. (Fifteen years later a few reconnaissance aircraft would have enabled the British to shadow the Boers on the open veld, thus profoundly altering the character of the war.) Nevertheless, by April, 1902, Kitchener could rely on the British Army to respond reasonably effectively, as had been proved during the preceding twelve months, when the numbers of combatant Boers was halved. This process of attrition was noted by Reitz. In August, 1901, he entered Cape Colony to join Smuts with ten comrades; four were caught and executed, either for being traitors or for wearing British uniform in place of their own rags, while six were wounded or captured. Reitz alone survived unscathed.

Kitchener's generalship was more open to the criticism that he directed the campaign in a too centralized manner. His working day began at 06.00 hours. His biographer wrote, 'After a close study of the messages his Staff shifted all the little flags on the maps which covered the whole floor, when "Chief" and Staff on hands and knees would set the positions of 30 or 40 columns on the maps. Kitchener then, telegrams in hand, dictated answers and fresh orders. After breakfast the heads of Supply, Transport, Railways and Ordnance Departments filed in, and with the detailed points of the night's cables and the exact positions of the columns in his hand, the "Chief" issued orders with unfailing accuracy.' Except for a short ride, Kitchener spent the rest of the day and evening immersed in administrative affairs. Beside his own small staff, his two closest collaborators, whom he saw daily, were Henderson, Chief Intelligence Officer, and Girouard, in charge of the railways.

Beside the cumulative strain induced by overwork, Kitchener's system had three serious defects. The first lay in the time-lag which elapsed between the intelligence reports arriving in his headquarters and orders being sent out, and, in rapidly changing situations, local commanders were sometimes prevented from striking a quick blow, or had to follow instructions that had become tactically meaningless. Secondly, Kitchener's tight control deprived his subordinates of the day-to-day responsibility rightly belonging to them; especially with more senior officers, this often led to un-questioning obedience replacing initiative. Ian Hamilton commented that Kitchener's idea of 'scientific warfare' was 'to carry on a conversation with his Generals right into the middle of the battle . . . Twice a day at least, and sometimes half a dozen times a day (he) gave them his orders'. Thirdly, Kitchener's isolation in Pretoria occasionally resulted in errors of judgement; he over-reacted to de Wet's invasion by transferring Paget's column from Transvaal, just before the drive there, so weakening this major operation.

Yet Kitchener's abilities far outweighed his deficiencies. As a relatively young, yet experienced soldier, he was extremely ambitious. Eager to take up his next post as Commander-in-Chief in India, he had a strong incentive for finishing the war as quickly as possible. He possessed the energy and self-confidence essential for galvanizing the British Army into that ceaseless activity so necessary for harrying guerrillas. It is also facile to blame Kitchener too severely for over-centralizing. Outbreaks of guerrilla activity being unpredictable and uncoordinated, firm central direction becomes paramount; otherwise a campaign can easily degenerate into chaos, with local commanders squabbling to obtain and to retain the limited resources available. Like all commanders-in-chief, Kitchener could but accept most of the senior officers who served under him. The performance of the majority of British generals in this war was unimpressive, none of them matching Kitchener's all-round professionalism, as even Milner had to admit. Contrary to some views, Kitchener was always anxious to discover and encourage outstanding ability; he gave French an almost free hand in Cape Colony, and backed Benson's unconventional night raids. Kitchener was always on the look-out for outstanding column commanders; Haig, Rawlinson, Gough, Plumer, Byng and Allenby gained invaluable experience in this rough, exhausting and often unrewarding school of war, and they could rely on Kitchener's support if they made the occasional mistake. Although Kitchener's handling of the campaign was not faultless, it cannot be overlooked that he brought the Boers to their knees, forcing them to sue for peace, which was no mean feat, as more recent guerrilla wars have conclusively shown.

Finally, Kitchener displayed considerable political acumen. He appreciated the fact that the wealthier Transvaalers were more susceptible to peace overtures than the Free Staters. Thus, on 7 March, with Landsdowne's approval, he sent the vague mediatory proposal from the Dutch Government to President Burger who was skulking in northeast Transvaal, having moved his seat of government 56 times in less than a year. As a result of this message, Burger requested and was granted safe conduct and an extraordinary series of talks began, to culminate, on 31 May, in the Peace of Vereeniging. The first problem was to persuade the main leaders to join Burger, but this proved easier than expected. On 9 April Botha came from the Natal border, and de Wet and de la Rey, accompanied by Steyn, met him at Klerksdorp. They soon moved to Pretoria and were joined by Milner. On

18 April, at Kitchener's suggestion, the delegates dispersed to carry out a referendum among the commandos who were to choose 30 representatives from each country.

Until 12 May, the war continued with large-scale drives in western Transvaal and north-eastern Orange Free State. But Kitchener no longer directed these himself, Ian Hamilton being responsible for operations in Transvaal and Bruce Hamilton in the Free State. Most opportunely for the British, on 11 April Kemp led a wild charge against Ian Hamilton's troops at Roodewall, losing 127 men. They would have lost far more had British rifle fire been more accurate. For the British these drives were disappointing, showing that, even without many of their most experienced leaders, the Boers were still formidable opponents. For the Boers, these offensives offered depressing evidence that they could expect no respite, even during the winter.

On 15 May the Transvaal and the Orange Free State Governments, each with their 30 delegates, foregathered at Vereeniging. The proceedings were prolonged and stormy. Burger, Botha and Smuts wanted peace immediately. With over 1,500 Transvaalers serving as National Scouts with the British Army and their numbers growing, with half the Uitlanders having returned and the gold mines working again, with the natives becoming increasingly hostile, with their women and children refused admission to the camps, with the prospect of more pacified areas being formed under the protection of Baden-Powell's South African Constabulary, where those loyal to Britain could be settled on empty farms and with nearly 25,000 prisoners of war in camps abroad, the Transvaal leaders knew that they and their followers could not much longer claim to be the sole representatives of their country. Smuts disposed of a hoary myth, asserting, 'there will be no general rising in the Cape Colony'. Botha's view was 'Let us do what we can to save our people even if we must lose our independence', and de la Rey eventually backed Botha and Smuts. Although both Steyn and de Wet had fled from the Free State to the Transvaalers they, and most of their followers, refused to submit. But on 29 May, Steyn resigned and went into hospital. After drafting an apologia for the war, de Wet, now in charge of the Free Staters, suddenly ended his opposition, and the peace terms were accepted by 54 votes to 6 on 31 May, 1902. These were lenient, including a guarantee that no rebels would be executed, and a British gift of £3 million to help restore the economy.

The delegates returned to their commandos to break the news. The men were assembled to hand over their rifles and take an oath of allegiance to Edward VII. Reitz wrote, 'This depressing ceremony was presided over by an English officer . . . with a regiment of troops in reserve close by. Despite his protests our men fired away their ammunition into the air, smashed their rifle-butts and sullenly flung the broken weapons down.' Reitz and his father refused to sign and went into voluntary exile. Jackson said somewhat nostalgically, 'The knowledge that no one would shoot at us from the next skyline made us feel quite neglected,' and concluded 'the place was alive with de la Rey's and Kemp's men coming in off commando, hobnobbing with Tommy in a most sociable way—men of every nationality.'

Thus lamely ended nearly two and a half years of war. During its course, the British had altogether to employ about 500,000 troops (including non-white armed scouts) against the Boers, whose forces never exceeded 70,000 and who, for most of the time, had less than 25,000 men in the field. Much of the Boer War was to be a foretaste of the sort of guerrilla warfare that professional armies have had to face increasingly during the twentieth century.

POSTSCRIPT

Most of the scars of war healed fairly quickly. The prisoners soon returned from their camps in Ceylon, Bermuda and St Helena. Assisted by the British Government's loan, economic recovery proceeded smoothly and Milner's rule, if not popular, was efficient. In 1910, the Boers gained their long-term aim when the Liberal administration granted independence to the four Colonies. Botha became the first Premier, Hertzog and Smuts were later to follow in his steps. But powerful and bitter memories still existed. These erupted in September, 1914, when, soon after Botha had joined Britain in declaring war on Germany, Christiaan de Wet and Kemp raised a short-lived rebellion, in the course of which de la Rey, perhaps the finest of the Boer leaders, was accidentally shot.

The Boer War aroused unprecedented public interest in the condition of the British Army and this, partly through Roberts' enthusiasm, continued unabated throughout the next decade. Reporting in 1903, the Elgin Commission analysed the lessons of the war, and heard the often conflicting evidence of main participants. The actual reforms began in 1904 when the Esher Committee issued its findings. The post of Commander-in-Chief was abolished, being replaced by the Army Council which, under the chairmanship of the Secretary of State for War, was made responsible to the Cabinet for all military affairs. The Esher Committee also recommended, and it was agreed, that the Committee of Imperial Defence be formed to advise on matters concerning joint service policy. In 1907, Haldane, Secretary of State for War, instituted a

General Staff, its first Chief being Lyttelton; Kitchener was offered, but refused, this appointment. Finally, the old voluntary organizations were superseded by the Territorial Army, mainly for home defence, which was based on 14 divisions, and the same number of mounted brigades. Although these and other reforms met with some opposition and scepticism, both the training and organization of the Army was greatly improved. Thus in August 1914 the British expeditionary field force of four divisions could be sent to France very rapidly, where it fought most effectively and as a properly constituted army. Unlike the Boer War, the major formations in the BEF in 1914 had exercised together and mostly remained under their peacetime commanders. Unfortunately, the Boer War had over-emphasized the importance of mounted troops as opposed to the artillery and the infantry and, as a result, a preponderance of the commanders were cavalrymen, including the mediocre French, the commander-in-chief of the BEF. Nevertheless, the British Army retreated skilfully from Mons to the Marne, inflicting heavy losses on the Germans who, based on its South African performances, discounted its fighting abilities. Without the Boer War, the British Army could never have evolved to become in 1914, one of the most efficient forces, for its size, in the world. Finally Kitchener emerged with enormously enhanced prestige. Although he had taken little interest in the defence reforms, the British public regarded him as almost a military genius. This faith in Kitchener's abilities was demonstrated by his being chosen, by general acclaim, as Secretary of State for War in August, 1914.

Chronological Table

Chronology of the Background to South African History

Background

1652	Dutch settled in Cape of Good Hope.
1814	British finally acquired Cape Colony from Holland.
1834–8	Abolition of Slavery.
1836	Start of Great Trek from the Cape to settle north of Orange River, Natal and across the Vaal River.
1843	Britain annexed Natal; most Boers migrated from there to Transvaal.
1852	Britain recognized Transvaal.
1854	Britain recognized Orange Free State.
1870	Diamond rush in Kimberley.
1877	Britain annexed Transvaal threatened by native uprisings and bankruptcy.
1880–1	First Boer War, Britain defeated at Majuba Hill, Britain granted self-government to Transvaal under Pretoria Convention, but retained vague suzerainty.
1883	Kruger elected President of Transvaal.
1884	London Convention. Transvaal renamed South African Republic (SAR) and obtained greater independence.
1884	Germans took over South-West Africa.
1885	Most of Bechuanaland annexed by Britain, blocking Boer penetration westwards.
1887	Zululand taken under British rule, blocking any Boer expansion coastwards in the east.
1890	With Britain's support, Rhodes' British South Africa Company began to settle Rhodesia, so called from 1895, blocking Boers to the north.
1895	Pretoria-Delagoa Bay railway opened to give SAR route to the coast not controlled by Britain.

1895	All British Bechuanaland placed under Cape Colony's rule.
1895	(Dec) Jameson Raid.
1897	Natal incorporated Zululand.
1897	Milner appointed High Commissioner.
1899	(May–June) Abortive Bloemfontein Conference between Kruger and Milner.
1899	(June) Britain reinforced her garrisons in South Africa.
1899	(9 Oct) Ultimatum, presented by Transvaal Government.

Phase I

THE BOER OFFENSIVE, THE BRITISH BESIEGED

1899

Oct	13	Boers invaded Natal
	14	Sieges of Kimberley and Mafeking started
	20	Battle of Talana
	21	Battle of Elandslaagte
	30	Battle of Lombard's Kop
	30	Siege of Ladysmith started
	31	Buller arrived at Cape Town

Phase II

BRITISH ATTEMPTS TO RELIEVE KIMBERLEY AND LADYSMITH

Nov	23	Battle of Belmont
	25	Battle of Graspan
	28	Battle of Modder River
Dec	10	Battle of Stormberg ⎫
	11	Battle of Magersfontein ⎬ Black Week
	15	Battle of Colenso ⎭
	17	Roberts appointed Commander-in-Chief

1900

Jan	6	Boer attack on Ladysmith
	10	Roberts arrived in Cape Town
	23/4	Battle of Spion Kop
Feb	5	Battle of Vaal Krantz

Phase III

BRITISH OFFENSIVES AND COLLAPSE OF ORGANIZED BOER RESISTANCE

Feb 15	Relief of Kimberley
27	Surrender of Cronje at Paardeberg
28	Ladysmith relieved
Mar 7	Battle of Poplar Grove
13	Bloemfontein captured
31	de Wet's successful ambush at Sannah's Post
May 3	Roberts began the march from Bloemfontein to Pretoria
31	Roberts entered Johannesburg
June 5	Roberts entered Pretoria
11	Battle of Diamond Hill
July 30	Prinsloo surrendered at Brandwater Basin
July/Aug	Burning of farms used by guerrilla fighters authorized
July/Aug	First de Wet hunt
Sept 11	Kruger fled to Europe
25	British reached Koomati Poort, the end of Delagoa Bay railway line

Phase IV

THE GUERRILLA WAR

Nov 29	Roberts finally handed over to Kitchener
Nov/Dec	Second de Wet hunt
Dec	Hertzog and Kritzinger entered Cape Colony
1901	
Jan/Feb	Third de Wet hunt
Mar/Apr	French's Transvaal drive
Mar	Middleburg Peace Conference between Kitchener and Botha
July	Smuts entered Cape Colony
Sept	Botha's attempted invasion of Natal
Oct 30	Benson killed
1902	
Jan/Feb	Large drives against de Wet in Orange Free State
Jan 25	Ben Viljoen captured
Mar 7	de la Rey captured Methuen at Tweebosch

Mar 23	Peace negotiations started
Apr 11	Kemp's defeat at Roodewall
May 30	Peace of Vereeniging signed. War cost Britain £220m.

The British Army Organization

Rank of Commanders

Division Commanders had the rank or local rank of Lieutenant-General. Brigade Commanders usually had the local rank of Major-General.

The Infantry Division

This usually consisted of Headquarters, an Engineer Company, and a Brigade Division of Artillery of 18 guns in three batteries, each having six 15 pounder guns and an ammunition column. Most of the troops were in the two (sometimes three) infantry brigades, each of four battalions. A battalion contained eight companies and its strength varied from 800 to 1,100 men.

Mounted Infantry

When Roberts took command all battalions that had arrived from home were ordered to provide a mounted infantry company—some did so by converting one of their eight companies, others made it a ninth company. All these companies were formed into 8 MI Bns. In April 1900, a reorganization of MI took place and they were formed into two Brigades.

Cavalry

This consisted of Headquarters, a Field troop of Engineers, two Brigades each of three cavalry regiments, and a Battery RHA. There were two 1st and 2nd Cav Bdes, one pair in the Cavalry Div under French, and the other operating under Buller in Natal.

Except for 15th Hussars, every regiment or corps in the British Army served in South Africa; in the case of some infantry regiments, only one of their two battalions was sent there.

Naval Brigades

They were drawn from sailors and marines stationed in South African waters and mostly served the guns removed from naval ships. The brigade with Methuen was over 400 strong and a small detachment with the large guns continued with Roberts to Pretoria. In Natal, the force was split and 283 went to Ladysmith, whilst 310 manned the naval guns during the battles that led to the relief of Ladysmith.

Order of Battle at the Time of the Advance into Transvaal, May, 1900

Commander-in-Chief—Field-Marshal Lord Roberts V.C., K.P.

Chief of Staff—Major-General Lord Kitchener

I. *FORCES EMPLOYED IN THE ORANGE FREE STATE AND TRANSVAAL*

    A. *The Main Army* starting from Bloemfontein area and advancing northwards.

        i. Central Column, under Roberts' personal command.

            Cavalry Division—Lieutenant-General J. D. P. French (on the left flank)

            1st Cavalry Brigade—Colonel T. C. Porter

            3rd   ,,   ,, —Brigadier-General J. R. P. Gordon

            4th   ,,   ,, —Major-General J. B. B. Dickson

            Strength 4,503 officers and men, 3,749 horses.

            1st Mounted Infantry Brigade—Major-General E. T. H. Hutton

            Four Corps of Mounted Infantry each commanded by a Colonel or Lieutenant-Colonel, Nos 4 and 8 Corps attached to 11 Division.

            Strength 4,315 officers and men, 4,508 horses.

            7th Division—Lieutenant-General C. Tucker

            14th Brigade—Major-General J. G. Maxwell

            15th   ,, —Major-General A. G. Wavell

Strength 7,167 officers and men, 635 horses (over half with artillery).

11th Division—Lieutenant-General R. Pole-Carew
1st Guards Brigade—Major-General Inigo Jones
18th Brigade—Brigadier-General T. E. Stephenson
Strength 7,805 officers and men, 668 horses.

Total Force (including Corps troops) 24,754 officers
and men
10,252 horses
66 field guns.

ii. Lieutenant-General Ian Hamilton's Force, on Roberts' right flank.

2nd Cavalry Brigade—Brigadier-General R. G. Broadwood

2nd Brigade Mounted Infantry—Brigadier-General C. P. Ridley

19th Brigade—Major-General H. L. Smith-Dorrien

21st Brigade—Major-General Bruce Hamilton

Supporting Column.

9th Division—Lieutenant-General Sir H. E. Colvile
3rd (Highland) Brigade—Major-General H. A. MacDonald

Total Force 18,627 officers and men
7,595 horses
48 field guns.

B. *Supporting Forces*, starting from Kimberley and moving north eastwards.

1st Division—Lieutenant-General Lord Methuen
9th Brigade—Major-General C. W. H. Douglas
20th Brigade—Major-General A. H. Paget
(3 Bns Imperial Yeomanry were attached).

10th Division—Lieutenant-General Sir A. Hunter
5th Brigade—Major-General A. FitzR. Hart
6th ,,   —Major-General G. Barton
(10th Division had been transferred from Natal).

C. *Static Formations*

3rd Division—Lieutenant-General Sir H. C. Chermside
22nd Brigade—Major-General R. E. Allen
23rd   „   —Major-General W. G. Knox (known as 'Nasty Knox')
This division held the line east of Bloemfontein. Mounted Infantry battalions were attached to it.

6th Division—Lieutenant-General T. Kelly-Kenny
12th Brigade—Major-General R. A. P. Clements
13th   „   —Major-General C. E. Knox (known as 'Nice Knox')
This division formed the Bloemfontein garrison.

D. *Back-up Formations*

8th Division—Lieutenant-General Sir H. M. L. Rundle
16th Brigade—Major-General B. B. D. Campbell
17th   „   —Major-General J. E. Boyes
This division's task was to move northwards from the Orange River to protect the rear of the main and supporting forces. Mounted Infantry battalions were attached to it.

Colonial Division—Brigadier-General E. Y. Brabant
This was composed mainly of South African troops and its strength was about half that of the cavalry division. Its task was to move on the eastern flank of 8th Division.

II. *FORCES EMPLOYED IN THE NATAL CAMPAIGN*

All formations started from Ladysmith area.

Commander—General Sir Redvers Buller

Cavalry. No over-all commander appointed.
1st Cavalry Brigade—Brigadier-General J. F. Burn-Murdoch
3rd   „   „   —Major-General J. F. Brocklehurst
3rd Mounted Brigade—Major-General Earl of Dundonald
This brigade was composed almost completely of South Africans.

2nd Division—Lieutenant-General C. F. Clery
2nd Brigade—Lieutenant-Colonel E. O. F. Hamilton
4th   ,,   —Colonel C. D. Cooper
4th Division—Lieutenant-General the Hon. N. G. Lyttelton
7th Brigade—Brigadier-General F. W. Kitchener
8th   ,,   —Major-General F. Howard
Most of the troops of this large division, over 10,500 strong, had been in the siege of Ladysmith and were unfit to take part in the advance into Transvaal.

5th Division—Lieutenant-General H. J. T. Hildyard
10th Brigade—Major-General J. T. Coke
11th   ,,   —Major-General A. S. Wynne

Total Force 45,715 officers and men
           11,653 horses
             113 field and 6 naval guns

III.   *SEPARATE FORCES*

A.   *Warren's Column*, quelling the remains of the revolt in Grinqualand (NW CapeColony) from May–July 1900.

Commander, Lieutenant-General Sir Charles Warren.

This was a mixed force less than a brigade strong, and was badly handled by Warren who was sent home after the revolt was ended.

B.   *Mafeking Relief Column*—Colonel B. T. Mahon
Strength about 1,100 mounted men mainly South Africans. It approached the town from the south.

C.   *Mafeking Garrison*—Colonel R. S. S. Baden-Powell
Strength 1,200 officers and men.

D.   *Plumer's Column*—Lieutenant-Colonel H. C. O. Plumer
Strength over 1,000, about half of whom were mounted. It operated north of Mafeking for most of the siege, but joined up with Mahon for the relief of the town

E.   *Rhodesian Field Force*—Lieutenant-General Sir F. Carrington
1st Brigade—Colonel G. A. L. Carew
2nd   ,,   —Colonel Raleigh Grey

Strength 4,000 mounted troops, nearly all of whom were
Australians and New Zealanders.

It operated along the Limpopo River on the northern
borders of Transvaal.

IV. *LINES OF COMMUNICATION FORCES*

Commander—Lieutenant-General Sir F. W. E. F. Forestier-
Walker

Strength, 23 Militia Battalions and Cape Colonial South
Africans protecting railway lines and bridges (see Kipling's
poem 'Bridge-guard in the Karroo').

V. *MISCELLANEOUS TROOPS*

Imperial Yeomanry, 10,000 strong formed into 20 battalions,
3 with the main army, 2 with the Rhodesian Field Forces
and 15 under training in Cape Colony.

Sick, about 20,000 in hospital.

Grand Total of troops 210,000. Sickness, training and other
causes reduced the numbers in the field to about 175,000.

By August, 1900, 265,132 troops had been sent to the war, of
whom 30,319 had been raised in South Africa and 11,584 had come
from other colonies.

Data of the Artillery Most Commonly Used in the Early Part of the Boer War

BRITISH ARMY

12 pdr, range 5,200 yds H.E. 3,800 yds shrapnel; 12½ lbs shell.
15 pdr, range 5,500 yds H.E. 4,100 yds shrapnel; 14 lbs shell.
5 in Howitzer, range 4,800 yds for both H.E. (Lyddite) and shrapnel; 50 lbs shell.

Naval guns removed from the cruisers *Terrible*, *Powerful*, *Monarch* and *Doris*.
12 pdr, range 8,000 yds H.E. only.
4·7 in, range 10,000 yds for both H.E. (Lyddite) and shrapnel; 45 lbs shell.

BOER

75 mm Creusot and Krupp, range 8,500 yds H.E. only; 14½ lbs shell.
115 mm Creusot, range 11,000 yds H.E. only; 88 lbs shell.

BOTH SIDES

1 pdr, 37 mm Maxim Vickers (Pom-Pom); range 3,000 yds.

High Explosive (H.E.) shells burst on impact; shrapnel are timed to burst in the air releasing 200 metal balls, which makes them very effective against troops in the open. The Boer shells often failed to explode, whilst Lyddite shells threw up impressive clouds of earth and smoke, but did little damage except where they actually landed.

The Organization of the Main British Artillery Formation

The personnel of a 15 pdr battery consisted of a major, a captain, 3 subalterns and 170 other ranks. Its 6 guns and limbers were each drawn by 6 horses; a gun and limber together weighed about $1\frac{3}{4}$ tons. With ammunition and other wagons and the riding horses, a battery had 138 horses. The Horse Artillery 12 pdr battery also had 6 guns, but a smaller establishment of men and horses. The Boers possessed no comparable organization, but their guns were very well handled, and they made good use of captured British guns. Finally, in this war the artillery played an increasingly minor and the horsed soldier an increasingly major role; the reverse was to be the case in the First World War.

Facts and Figures relating to the Boer War

Duration   11 October, 1899—31 May, 1902

Areas

United Kingdom (inc. N. Ireland)	94,207 sq. miles		
England	50,327 ,, ,,		
Orange Free State	50,396 ,, ,,		
Transvaal (South African Republic)	111,196 ,, ,,		
Cape Colony (excluding Bechuanaland)	258,000 ,, ,, (approx.)		
Natal	35,371 ,, ,,		

Distances

Southampton—Cape Town	6,000 miles		
Cape Town—Durban	812	sea miles	
,, ,, —de Aar	501	rail ,,	
,, ,, —Kimberley	647	,, ,,	
,, ,, —Bloemfontein	750	,, ,,	
,, ,, —Pretoria	1,040	,, (equal to Berlin–Rome)	
Durban—Ladysmith	189	,, miles	
,, —Newcastle	268	,, ,,	
,, —Pretoria	511	,, ,,	
Port Elizabeth—Bloemfontein	450	,, (equal to London–Perth)	
,, ,, —Pretoria	740	,, miles	
Pretoria—Koomati Poort	291	,, ,,	

Populations

United Kingdom (inc. N. Ireland)	44·5m (1901 Census)	
Transvaal (white inhabitants)	approx. 300,000 (no census till 1904)	

Orange Free State	(white inhabitants)	approx. 145,000
		(no census till 1904)
Cape Colony	,,	,,	approx. 579,000
		(based on 1904 census)
Natal	,,	,,	approx. 97,000

Cost to Britain approx. £220 m.

British Troops who served in South Africa. Grand total 448,435 (Figures from *Official History*, Vol IV).

Breakdown of grand total (to nearest 500):

a. *Regulars* (including Reservists), 256,000;
cavalry=27,000; artillery=21,000; infantry=175,000;
staffs and others=33,000.
At the outbreak of war the Regular white troops=227,000. About 126,000 Regular recruits joined the Army during the war the net annual gain being 13,500 over the previous 7 years. The Reservists=83,000. These men were liable to recall from civilian life for up to 9 years and their fitness for military service varied, as did their girth, that caused some 'kitting-out' problems.

b. *Militia* 45,500. They were attached to Regular battalions as reinforcements. Their engagement was for six years and they had to attend an initial six weeks' training period and a 28-day camp each year. Over half the Militia were youths under 19 who intended joining the Regulars when they had reached the required medical standards. About 105,000 joined the Militia in the Boer War.

c. *Yeomanry* 36,500

d. *Volunteers* 20,000

The Volunteers and the Yeomanry were originally to be employed only for home defence, but in January, 1900, to circumvent this restriction new units were formed out of existing ones, being known as Imperial Yeomanry. These troops were usually keen amateurs and had had little or no proper training. About 92,000 men enlisted in these formations.

e. *South African Constabulary* 8,500, including over 1,200 raised in Canada.

f. *Colonials* over 29,000; 16,715 Australians, 6,400 New Zealanders, 6,000 Canadians.

g. *Raised in South Africa* approx. 52,000.

Minimum official age for service overseas 20.

Work of Sea Transport
Personnel sent to South Africa=386,081.
Horses sent to South Africa=352,864 of which over 280,000 were remounts, 73,000 coming from UK, 97,000 from USA, 45,000 from Austria-Hungary, 26,000 from Argentine, 25,000 from Australia, 14,000 from Canada and about 3,000 from India. Costs per cob and horse average UK £29–£43, USA £17–£25, Hungary £20–£35, Australia £10–£14, Argentine £8, Canada £25–£30. Mules sent to South Africa=104,000, over 75,000 from USA costing £12–£15 each approx and 20,000 from Spain £20 each, and 8,000 from Italy at £20–£22.
Stores sent=1,374 m tons exclusive of troops' equipment, etc. accompanying them or supplies from outside UK.
Ships engaged=1,027.

The Butcher's Bill. There are discrepancies between the *Official History* and *The Times* Vol VII, whose figures are in brackets:

BRITISH FORCES

a. *Total Deaths*=20,721 (21,942 but including 800 accidental). Casualty breakdowns:
Killed in action or of wounds=7,582 including 712 officers (7,894; 706 officers);
Died of disease=13,139 including 406 officers (13,250; 339 officers).
(In World War I the King's Royal Rifle Corps raised 17 battalions and lost 13,000 killed and 123,000 wounded.)

b. *Total Casualties* from all causes including wounded=52,150. Highest regimental casualties; both served from November, 1899, to the end of the war:
2nd Royal Lancasters; 11 officers, 128 other ranks (at Spion Kop and relief of Ladysmith).

2nd Royal Highlanders (Black Watch); 12 officers, 119 other
ranks (Magersfontein and Paardeberg).
South African forces killed=1,473, including 119 officers.
South African forces died of disease=1,607, including 69
officers. Australians=518 killed. New Zealanders=228
killed. A comparison—2nd Rifle Brigade=75 killed
(7 officers) in Boer War (Oct 1899–May 1902); Aug 1914–
Dec 1916=816 killed (42 officers). Strangest statistics, 1st
Connaught Rangers, no officers but 58 other ranks killed.

c. *Battles with casualties of over 1,000*
Relief of Ladysmith 19–27 Feb, 356 killed, 1,536 wounded,
5 prisoners.
Spion Kop, 403 killed, 1,054 wounded, 303 prisoners.
Paardeberg, 16–27 Feb, 348 killed, 1,133 wounded, 59
prisoners (nearly all on first day).
Lombards Kop, 76 killed, 342 wounded, 968 prisoners.
Colenso, 171 killed, 738 wounded, 197 prisoners.

BOER FORCES

Grand Total engaged=87,365, *Official History*.
a. *Boer Casualties*, killed in action=4,000 estimated, *Official History* gives no figures for this category.

b. *Boer Prisoners* in camps, mainly abroad=26,000. June, 1902.

c. *Boer Ex-Combatants* on parole, in refugee camps or died=
7,347. June, 1902.

d. *Boer Forces in the Field*=20,779, of whom 3,574 were
rebels and 140 foreigners. June, 1902.

The *Official History* figures for combatants is unsatisfactory,
leaving about 20,000 unaccounted for. It is improbable that more
than 10,000 either surrendered and returned home, or went into
exile in Mozambique, thus *The Times* total of 65,000 having fought
with the Boers seems a reasonable estimate.

Concentration Camps

1902 average population=114,000 (approx.) of whom about
95,000 were women and children.
Also approx. 100,000 natives were in camps.
It is estimated that 20,000 Boer inmates of these camps died
between September, 1900, and June, 1902. Most of the deaths
occurred in the early part of this period.

South African Medals and Clasps

Clasps on Queen's Medals:

> Belfast
> Belmont
> Cape Colony
> Diamond Hill
> Driefontein
> Elandslaagte
> Johannesburg
> Defence of Kimberley
> Relief of Kimberley
> Defence of Ladysmith
> Relief of Ladysmith
> Laing's Nek
> Defence of Mafeking
> Relief of Mafeking
> Modder River
> Natal
> Orange Free State
> Paardeberg
> Rhodesia
> Talana
> Transvaal
> Tugela Heights
> Wepener
> Wittebergen

Clasps on King's Medals:

> South Africa, 1901
> South Africa, 1902

Selected Bibliography

BOOKS PUBLISHED BEFORE 1910

(i) Main Sources

The Times History of the War in South Africa. 7 Vols. Edited by L. S. Amery. Sampson Low, Marston and Co. 1902–9. By far the best and fullest account. Vol. I deals with South Africa before the war, Vol. VI largely covers the years immediately after the war, while Vol. VII is mainly index, but includes 30 pages of bibliography.

Official History of the War in South Africa. 4 Vols. Hurst and Blackett 1906–10. Vols. I and II by Maj.-Gen. Sir Frederick Maurice. Vols. III and IV by H. Grant and others. With four volumes of maps.

Report of the Royal Commission on the War in South Africa. (Elgin Commission) 1903. 4 Vols. Cd 1789–92 H.M.S.O.

German Official Account of the War in South Africa. 2 Vols. Murray 1904–6. Vol. I trans. by Col. W. H. Waters. Vol. II March-Sept. 1900 trans. by Col. H. Du Cane.

(ii) Secondary Sources

Abbott, J. H. M. *Tommy Cornstalk* (An Australian View). Longmans 1902.

Blake, Col. J. Y. F. *A West Pointer with the Boers.* Boston 1903.

Burleigh, Bennet. *The Natal Campaign.* Chapman and Hall 1900.

Churchill, Winston. *Frontier Wars.* Sections entitled *London to Ladysmith* and *Ian Hamilton's March.* Eyre and Spottiswoode 1962.

Crowe, George. *Commission of H.M.S. Terrible.* Newnes 1903.

De Wet, C. R. *Three Years' War.* Constable 1903.

Doyle, A. Conan. *The Great Boer War.* Smith and Elder 1901–2.

Goldman, C. S. *With General French and the Cavalry in South Africa.* Macmillan 1902.

James, Lionel (published under 'Intelligence Officer'). *On the Heels of De Wet*. Blackwood 1902.

Kipling, Rudyard. *The Five Nations*. (poems) Methuen 1903.

Kruger, S. J. P. *Memoirs of Paul Kruger*. Fisher Unwin 1902.

Mahan, Capt. A. T. *Story of the War in South Africa*. Sampson Low 1900. Reprinted 1973 Westport Publications Ltd.

Rankin, R. (published under Anonymous). *A Subaltern's Letters to his Wife*. Longmans 1901.

Reitz, D. *Commando*. Faber and Faber 1967 (paperback).

Sternberg, Count. *My Experiences of the Boer War*. Longmans 1901. (Translated by Lt.-Col. G. F. R. Henderson).

Viljoen, Ben. *My Reminiscences of the Anglo-Boer War*. Hood, Douglas and Howard 1902.

Villebois D. Mareuil, Count G. H. de. *War Notes*. Trans. by F. Lees. A. & C. Black 1902.

Wallace, Edgar. *Unofficial Despatches on the Boer War*. Hutchinson 1901–2.

Wilson, H. W. *With the Flag to Pretoria*. 2 Vols. Harmsworth 1900–1.

Wilson, H. W. *After Pretoria, the Guerilla War*. 2 Vols. Amalgamated Press. 1902

BOOKS PUBLISHED AFTER 1910

Amery, J. *Life of Joseph Chamberlain*. Vol. IV. Macmillan 1961.

Arthur, Sir G. *Life of Lord Kitchener*. Vols. I and II. Macmillan 1920.

Callwel, Maj.-Gen. *Field Marshal Sir Henry Wilson*. Vol. I Cassell 1927.

Curtis, L. *With Milner in South Africa*. Blackwell 1951.

Dundonald, Earl of. *My Army Life*. Arnold 1926.

Fitzpatrick, Sir Percy. *South African Memories*. Cassell 1932.

Fuller, J. F. C. *The Last of the Gentlemen's Wars*. Faber & Faber 1937.

Gardner, B. *Allenby*. Cassell 1965.

Hancock, W. K. *Smuts*. Vol. I. Cambridge 1962.

Jackson, M. C. *A Soldier's Diary*. Goschen 1913.

James, D. *Lord Roberts*. Hollis and Carter 1954.

Johnson, D. *Anglo-Boer War*. Jackdaw No. 68 (Cape).

Kruger, R. *Goodbye Dolly Grey*. Nel Mentor (paperback) 1967.

Lyttelton, Gen. Sir N. *Eighty Years*. Hodder & Stoughton 1927.

Marais, J. P. S. *Fall of Kruger's Republic*. Oxford 1961.

Martin, A. C. *The Concentration Camps*. Howard Timmins Cape Town 1958.

Maurice, Maj.-Gen. Sir F. *Rawlinson*. Cassell 1923.

Meintjes, J. *General Louis Botha*. Cassell 1970.

Pemberton, W. B. *Battles of the Boer War*. Pan Books 1969.

Sampson V. and Hamilton. I. *Anti-Commando*. Faber 1931.

Selby, J. *The Boer War*. Barker 1969.

Smith-Dorrien, Gen. Sir H. *Memories of 48 Years Service*. Murray 1925.

Symons, J. *Buller's Campaign*. Cresset Press 1963.

INDEX

In most cases, the British ranks are those held in May, 1900.
Cmdt. = Commandant. The contemporary spelling of place names
sometimes varies, e.g. Koodoos or Koodoes.

175